Christmas
in
My Heart

A TIMELESS TREASURY
OF HEARTWARMING STORIES

Christmas

in

My Heart

Compiled and Edited by

JOE WHEELER

Guideposts®

CARMEL, NEW YORK 10512

www.guidepostsbooks.com

THIS GUIDEPOSTS EDITION IS PUBLISHED BY SPECIAL
ARRANGEMENT WITH DOUBLEDAY
a division of Bantam Doubleday Dell Publishing
Group, Inc.

Book Design by Jennifer Ann Daddio

Library of Congress Cataloging-in-Publication Data
Christmas in my heart. Selections
Christmas in my heart: a timeless treasury of heartwarming
stories   /   [compiled   and   edited   by]
Joe Wheeler.— 1st ed.
p.   cm.
Selections of the short stories included in the
edition published by Review and Herald Pub.
Associates, c1992–c1995.
1. Christmas stories, American. I. Wheeler, Joe L.,
1936– . II. Title.
PS648.C45C4472   1996
813'.010833—dc20   96–25672
                                                  CIP

ISBN 0-385-48567-0

Acknowledgments

Introduction: "Once Upon A Christmas" by Joseph Leininger Wheeler. Copyright © 1996 by Joseph Leininger Wheeler. Printed by permission of the author.

"The Last Straw" by Paula Palangi McDonald. Copyright © 1979 by Paula Palangi McDonald. Published in *Family Circle/Women's Day*, December 1979. Published as a separate book by David C. Cook, 1992. Reprinted by permission of the author.

"The Jubilee Agreement" by Terry Beck. Copyright © 1990 by Terry Beck. Published in *Virtue Magazine*, November–December 1992. Reprinted by permission of the author.

"Trouble at the Inn" by Dina Donohue. Reprinted by permission from *Guideposts Magazine*, copyright © 1966 by Guideposts, Carmel, NY 10512.

Contents

Once Upon A Christmas

INTRODUCTION

"Once upon a time" . . . any self-respecting fairy tale begins there. Born as they are in the folk-consciousness of a people, fairy tales deal not with externals but with the basics, with the wellsprings of our thoughts and actions. The same is true of the Christmas story in its countless variations. The good ones—the ones that refuse to die—are almost primitive in their simplicity and lack of subterfuge. And they are unabashedly sentimental.

Of all the times in the year when sentiment prevails, none exceeds Christmas. Undoubtedly, the time of year helps. The nights are getting longer, the air is cold and crisp, snow flocks city and county streets with ermine, the pace of life slows just a little, and the low temperatures make us more aware of the presence or absence of human warmth, in whatever form it may manifest itself. It's hard to imagine us singing Christmas carols in the sweltering heat of July, for instance. Somehow nature, tradition, and coincidental good timing joined forces to bring us this most special of all days at just the right time of year.

Christmas is family time . . . thus at no time in the year are the survivors of death or separation more likely to be racked by waves of loneliness. And let's face it, sadly, many of us are very "Lonely." We are a culture of isolated individuals pretending to be happily self-sufficient, but we are getting lonelier. We try to block out just how lonely we are with all sorts of artificial barricades: television, radio, chatter, movies, videos, activity, liquor, drugs, sports; and most of the year we succeed fairly well. Except at Christmas. For some reason the normal defenses simply don't work at

Christmas. When you can't go home at Christmas you realize just how dead-end and lacking in substance or meaning life is, as evidenced in the increased holiday-season suicide rate.

One of the greatest tragedies of our time is the shattering of the family unit; without it, no nation has flourished long on this planet. Television and the mass media have replaced the family and God as the centers of our society. When Christ-less programming of the child's ethical framework takes the place of God and value-centered home and church programming, the result is a lost generation.

But all is not lost. And one of the solutions to our dilemma is to rediscover the enduring "Once Upon A Christmas" values, recognizing that a society—or a family—divorced from God can do nothing but self-destruct.

Again, we come back to sentiment. One can no more truly experience Christmas in all its dimensions without emotion than one can fall in love on a purely rational plane. Part of the loveliness of Christmas lies in this melodious interplay of love, caring, laughter, tears, forgiveness, empathy, and healing among the strings of our souls. The awesome power of great Christmas stories is that they make us laugh or cry, uplift our spirit, radically change our behavior patterns so that we may begin life anew.

One of the earliest and fondest memories of my childhood has to do with these stories that touch the heart. Often I wing my way backward through time by recalling the *real* tree, the *real* caring, the *real* people, the *real* relationships with others and God that these "Once Upon A Christmas" stories revealed.

And when I see these scenes flashed on my memory's video screen again, almost invariably, there she is: Mother. An elocutionist of the old school, Mother knew the great stories almost by heart. Those great ones that never grew old, no matter how many times we had heard them before. We knew them practically by heart ourselves: We knew when the funny parts were nearing . . . and we knew by Mother's slowing pace that she was going to cry. It was stories such as these that painted individual Christmas canvases with such vivid colors. So timeless and precious are these stories that no sacrifice is too much, no cost too great, to pay in order to go "home for Christmas" and hear those cathartic stories once again. They give meaning to love, family, home, and God—they bring the real Christmas into focus.

It all started so innocently, so casually, one cold winter evening on Maryland's Severn River. Inside, the fire was blazing in the weathered brick fireplace, and I had collapsed in an easy chair after a hard week. One of my students and I were talking. We spoke of many things — I can't remember what—but I *do* remember her question: "Dr. Wheeler, have you ever thought of writing a Christmas story?" Not accustomed to this role reversal, I, the teacher, reluctantly took on the role of student. I got up out of my easy chair and searched for paper and my black Pilot pen (my muse—it *only* unlocks my ideas), then sat down and started dreaming up a story. From time to time during that weekend, I shoved a page under her nose and asked for input. Thus was born my first Christmas story, "The Snow of Christmas."

About two years later, my first collection of Christmas stories (published by Review & Herald) hit the market, and I lost control of my life. I became prisoner of this long pent-up need for a different kind of Christmas story. For each of the last three Christmas seasons, Dr. James Dobson of Focus on the Family has chosen a *Christmas in My Heart* story to anchor his Christmas message of the year, hence the stories have been read by untold millions as a result.

Out of all this, Dr. Mark Fretz, senior religion editor for Doubleday noticed the stories. So deeply moved was he by what he read that together we have raced this manuscript to press in time for the 1996 Christmas season.

Providentially, I have been collecting stories all my life. In recent years, however, all across the United States and Canada, readers have decided to keep my feet to the fire by inundating me with wave after wave of stories, stories that are so old they are crumbling into fragments. Not a moment too soon did I begin this ministry of bringing them back!

Unquestionably, the golden age of Christmas stories occurred during the first third of this century; actually, it began in the 1890s and receded during the forties. Clearly, this was a period of spiritual renewal in America . . . and, not surprisingly, it parallels the Social Gospel Period. This was born with Charles Sheldon's *In His Steps* in 1898 and flowered with Harold Bell Wright's Trilogy: *That Printer of Udel's, The Calling of Dan Matthews,* and *God and the Groceryman.* These authors held a deep conviction that the essence of Christianity is not sterile doctrine, but the application of Biblical principles into a caring relationship with all those with whom we come in contact on a daily basis.

Now again, at century's end, Christmas and fam-

❖

ilies and caring are becoming special. During the holidays you see families making more of an attempt to get together. Paradoxically, in an age when one out of every two marriages ends in divorce, you see an almost feverish attempt to corral the few shreds of family that remain.

Which brings us to orphans. Interestingly enough, a surprisingly large number of the memorable Christmas stories deal with orphans. Today, orphans in the traditional sense are vastly outnumbered by "orphans" who are deprived of adult love and protection by divorce. Let's face it: The results are almost indistinguishable. In fact, it oft appears that divorce may be more traumatic—no matter what the age—than physical death. I am reminded of one of the most moving open letters I have ever read, a letter that was addressed to the editor of a large metropolitan newspaper. The writer was a middle-aged woman whose senior-citizen parents had recently divorced, the father having found someone younger and more attractive. The writer observed that the resulting loss of a family center came home to roost every Christmas because there was no longer any home to go to. Mom was alone—embittered and impoverished—in a small apartment; Dad and his new live-in represented a totally alien world, a world that the daughter and family felt was antithetical to their values.

So utterly lost did she feel, in a moral sense, that she found herself, even at middle age, floundering in a sea of doubt, unable to find bedrock anywhere.

There is a crucial difference between Christmas stories that merely entertain and those that touch the heart. I have seen a number of anthologies of Christmas stories for sale, and bought them——on the strength of the title or reviews, all of which trumpeted the news that they were "great" Christmas stories——only to discover that the bulk (if not all) of them, although technically well written, although featuring some of the most famous names of our age, lacked that one ingredient I consider absolutely essential: touching the heart itself. Without this intangible variable, I personally refuse to grant an accolade such as "great" to any story, no matter how much of a highflier the author is, and no matter how well written the story may be from a literary point of view.

The other side of the coin is that from a purely technical point of view, a number of the stories I have included in this treasury are flawed, nevertheless I included them because of their emotive and convicting power.

MY DREAM

It is my sincere hope that this collection of stories (culled from thousands) will represent more than shelf fodder to you, that the characters in these stories will become old friends—to be taken down and shared with your family and friends every Christmas season. I included only those stories that I have shared with others enough to be certain of their power.

Most important of all, however, there was one factor motivating me finally, after all these years, to take the time to select the pure gold of the collection for publication. That was the conviction that there is such a great need today for Christ-centered Christmas stories that will remind us, every time we read one, that this is really what Christmas—and life itself—is all about. Without it, Christmas is but a hollow drum beaten by commercial opportunists, or to paraphrase Shakespeare, "a tale, told by an idiot, full of sophistry and futility, signifying *nothing*."

I have taken occasional editorial liberties: updating words or terms that have become archaic or have acquired negative connotations.

Welcome to the timeless world of Christmas.

CODA

Each reader of this collection can make a difference. If enough readers respond positively to the collection and communicate their reactions to me, we will consider putting together additional collections of stories—there are so many splendid ones I had to leave out! (And, if you know the earliest origin or true authorship of a story we have not been able to track to its source, please relay that to us so we can correct it before another printing.) Furthermore, I am positive that some of the greatest stories haven't even been found yet; thus I hope that each of you will search for them and take the time to send me copies of the best ones for possible inclusion in the next collection (be sure to include author, publisher, and date, if possible). You may contact me at the following address:

Joe L. Wheeler, Ph.D.
c/o Doubleday Religion Department
1540 Broadway
New York, New York 10036

The Last Straw

❖

PAULA PALANGI MCDONALD

The McDonalds have discovered the joy of Christmas, but they don't see the true meaning until they reach the last straw.

❖ ❖ ❖

"The Last Straw" is a true story that you can incorporate into your Christmas. It's easy. Even children as young as three can understand giving in secret and participate enthusiastically. "The Last Straw" offers a way to bring back the true spirit and meaning of Christmas.

It changed forever the way our family prepared our hearts for Christmas. It can change yours, too. All you really need is a handful of straw.

——Paula Palangi McDonald

It was another long winter afternoon with everyone stuck in the house. And the four little McDonalds were at it again—bickering, teasing, fighting over their toys.

At times like these, Mother was almost ready to believe that her children didn't love each other, even though she knew that wasn't really true. All brothers and sisters fight, of course, but lately her little bunch had been particularly horrible to one another, especially Eric and Kelly, who were just a year apart. They seemed determined to spend the whole long winter making each other miserable. Pick, pick, pick. Squabble, squabble, squabble.

"Gimme that. It's mine!"

"Is not, fatso! I had it first!"

Mother sighed as she listened to the latest argument coming from the living room. With Christmas only a month away, the McDonald house seemed sadly lacking in Christmas spirit. This was supposed to be the season of sharing and love, of warm feelings and happy hearts. But where were those warm feelings and happy hearts? A home needed more than just pretty packages or twinkling lights on a tree to fill it with the Christmas spirit. But how could any mother convince her children that being kind to each other was the most important way to get ready for Christmas?

Mother had only one idea. Years ago her grandmother had told her about an old custom that helped people discover the real meaning of Christmas. Perhaps it would work for her family this year. It was certainly worth a try.

Mother gathered her four little rascals together and sat them down on the stairs, smallest to tallest—Mike, Randi, Kelly, and Eric. "How would you kids like to start a new Christmas project this year?" she asked. "It's like a game, but it can only be played by people who can keep a secret. Can everyone here do that?"

"I can!" shouted Eric, wildly waving his arm in the air.

"I can keep a secret better than he can!" yelled Kelly, jumping up and waving her arms in the air, too. If there was going to be any kind of a contest, Kelly wanted to make sure she beat Eric.

"I can do it!" chimed in Randi, not quite sure what was happening but not wanting to be left out either.

"Me too, me too, me too," squealed little Mike, bouncing up and down. "I'm big enough."

"Well then, here's how the game works," Mother explained. "This year we're going to surprise baby Jesus when He comes on Christmas Eve by making Him the softest bed in the world. We're going to build a little crib for Him to sleep in right here in our house and fill it with straw to make it comfortable. But here's the secret part. The straw we put in the manger will measure all the kind things we do between now and Christmas. We just can't tell anyone who we're doing the good things for."

The children look confused. "But how will baby Jesus know it's His bed?"

"He'll know," said Mother. "He'll recognize it by the love we put in it to make it soft. And He'll be happy to sleep there."

"But who will we do the kind things for?" asked Eric, who was still a little confused.

"It's simple," said Mother. "We'll do them for each other. Once every week between now and Christmas, we'll put all of our names in this hat, mine and Daddy's, too. Then we'll do kind things for the person whose name we get for a whole week. But here's the hard part. We can't tell anyone else whose name we draw for that week. We'll each try to do as many favors for our special person as we can without getting caught. And for every secret good thing we do, we'll put another straw in the crib."

"Like being a spy!" squealed Randi. "I can do that! I'm a good spy."

"But what if I pick someone who I don't like?" said Kelly, frowning.

Mother thought about that for a minute. "Maybe you could use extra fat straws for those good things because they just might be harder to do. And think how much faster the fat straws will fill up our crib. Then on Christmas Eve we'll put baby Jesus in His little bed, and He'll sleep that night on a mattress made of love. I think He'd like that, don't you?

"Now, who will build a little crib for us?" she asked.

Eric was the oldest and the only one allowed to use the tools alone, so he marched off to the basement to try. There were banging noises and sawing noises, and for a long time there were no noises at all. But finally, Eric climbed back up the stairs with a proud smile. "The best crib in the world!" He grinned. "And I did it all myself."

For once, everyone agreed. The little manger *was* the best crib in the world, even though one leg was an inch too short and the crib rocked a bit. But it had been built with love—and about a hundred bent nails—so it would certainly last a long time.

"Now we need straw," said Mother, and together they tumbled out to the car to go looking for some.

Surprisingly, no one fought over who was going to sit in the front seat that day as they drove around searching for an empty field. At last they spotted a small vacant lot that had been covered with tall grass in the summer. Now that it was December, the dried, yellow stalks looked just like real straw.

Mother stopped the car, and even though it was a bitter-cold day, the kids scrambled out to pick handfuls of the tall grass.

"That's enough!" Mother finally laughed when the cardboard box in the trunk was almost overflowing. "Remember, it's only a small crib." So home they went to spread their straw carefully on a tray Mother had put on the kitchen table. The empty manger was placed gently on top, and no one could even notice that it had one short leg.

"When can we pick names? When can we pick?" shouted the children, their faces still rosy from the cold.

"As soon as Daddy comes home for dinner," Mother answered.

At the supper table that night, the six names were written on separate pieces of paper, folded up, shuffled and shaken around in an old baseball hat, and the drawing began.

Kelly picked first and immediately started to giggle. Randi reached into the hat next, trying hard to look like a serious spy. Daddy glanced at his scrap of paper and smiled quietly behind his hand. Mother picked out a name, but her face never gave away a clue. Next, little Mike reached into the hat, but since he couldn't read yet, Daddy had to whisper in his ear and tell him which name he had picked. Mike then quickly ate his little scrap of paper so that no one would ever find out who his secret person was. Eric was the last to choose, and as he unfolded his piece of paper, a frown crossed his face. But he stuffed the name quickly into his pocket and said nothing. The family was ready to begin.

The week that followed was filled with surprises. It seemed the McDonald house had suddenly been invaded by an army of invisible elves, and good things were happening everywhere. Kelly would walk into her room at bedtime and find her little blue nightgown neatly laid out and her bed turned down. Someone had cleaned up the sawdust under the workbench without being asked. The jelly blobs disappeared magically from the kitchen counter after lunch one day while Mother was out getting the mail. And every morning while Eric was brushing his teeth, someone crept quietly into his room and made his bed. It wasn't made perfectly, but it was made. That particular little elf must have had very short arms because he couldn't seem to reach all the way to the middle.

"Where are my shoes?" asked Daddy one morning. No one seemed to know, but before he left for work, they were back in the closet, all shined up.

Mother noticed other changes during that week, too. The children weren't teasing or fighting as much. An argument would start and then suddenly stop right in the middle for no apparent reason. Even Eric and Kelly seemed to be getting along better and bickering less. In fact, all the children could be seen smiling secret smiles and giggling to themselves at times. And slowly, one by one, pieces of straw began to appear in the little crib. At first there were just a few, but then a few more appeared each day. By the end of the first week, there was actually a little pile in the crib. Now, mind you, no one ever saw the straws go in, but later the children could be seen patting and testing the tiny pile for softness.

By Sunday everyone was anxious to pick new names again, and this time there were more laughter and merriment during the picking process than there had been the first time, except for Eric. Once again he unfolded his piece of paper, looked at it, and stuffed it in his pocket without a word. Mother noticed, as mothers always do, but said nothing.

The second week brought more amazing events! The garbage was taken out without anyone's being asked. Someone even did two of Kelly's hard math problems one night when she left her homework out on the table.

The little pile of straw grew higher and softer. Everyone seemed to be watching and checking it carefully each day. With only two weeks left until Christmas, the children wondered if their homemade bed would be comfortable enough for baby Jesus when He came.

"Who will be baby Jesus anyway?" Randi asked on the third Sunday night after they had all picked new names. "What can we use?"

"Perhaps we can use one of the dolls," said Mother. "Why don't you and Mike be in charge of picking out the right one?"

The two youngest children ran off to gather up their favorite dolls, but everyone else wanted to help pick baby Jesus, too. Little Mike dragged his Bozo the Clown rag doll from his room and proudly handed it over, sniffling later when everybody laughed. Soon Eric's well-hugged teddy bear, Bruffles, joined the dolls filling up the couch. Barbie and Ken were there, along with Kermit the Frog, a pile of soft stuffed dogs and lambs, and even a cuddly monkey that Grandma and Grandpa had sent Mike one year. But none of them seemed quite right.

Only an old baby doll, who had been loved almost to pieces, looked like a possibility for their baby Jesus. Chatty Baby she had once been called, before she stopped chatting forever after too many baths.

"But she looks funny now," said Randi. And it was true; she did look funny. Once, while playing beauty shop, Kelly had cut her own blond hair along with Chatty Baby's, giving them both a raggedy crew cut. Kelly's hair had eventually grown back, but Chatty Baby's never had, and now the wisps of blond hair that stuck out all over her head made her look a little lost and forgotten. But her eyes were still bright blue and she still smiled, even though her face was slightly smudged from the touch of so many chubby little fingers.

"I think she's perfect," said Mother. "Baby Jesus probably didn't have much hair when He was born ei-

❖

ther. And I'll bet He'd like to be represented by a doll who's had so many hugs."

So it was decided, and the children began to make a new outfit for their baby Jesus—a little leather vest out of scraps and some cloth diapers, because none of them quite knew what swaddling clothes were supposed to look like. But baby Jesus looked just fine in His new clothes, and best of all, He fit perfectly into the little crib. Since it wasn't quite time for Him to sleep there yet, He was laid carefully on a shelf in the hall closet to wait for Christmas Eve and a softer bed.

Meanwhile, the pile of straw grew and grew. Every day brought new and different surprises as the secret elves stepped up their activity. There was more laughter around the house, as well as less teasing and hardly any meanness. The McDonald home was finally filled with the Christmas spirit. Only Eric had been unusually quiet since the third week of name picking, and sometimes Mother would catch him looking a little sad and unhappy. But the straw in the manger continued to pile up.

At last it was almost Christmas. The final Sunday night of name picking was the night before Christmas Eve. As the family sat around the table waiting for the last set of names to be shaken in the hat, Mother said, "You've all done a wonderful job. There must be hun-

23

dreds of straws in our crib—maybe a thousand. You should be so pleased with the bed you've made. But remember, there's still one whole day left. We all have time to do a little more to make the bed even softer before tomorrow night. Let's try."

The children smiled as they looked at their fluffy pile of straw. No one needed to test it anymore. They all knew it was comfortable and soft. But maybe they could still make it a little deeper, a little softer. They were going to try.

For the last time the hat was passed around the table. Little Mike picked out a name, Daddy whispered it to him, then Mike quickly ate the paper just as he had done every week. Randi unfolded hers carefully under the table, peeked at it, and then hunched up her little shoulders, smiling. Kelly reached into the hat and giggled happily when she saw the name. Mother and Dad each took their turns, too, before handing the hat with the last name to Eric. But as he unfolded the small scrap of paper and read it, his face pinched up and he suddenly seemed about to cry. Without a word, he turned and ran from the room.

Everyone immediately jumped from the table, but Mother stopped them. "No! Stay where you are," she said. "Let me talk to him alone first."

Just as she reached to the top of the stairs, Eric's

door banged open. He was trying to pull his coat on with one hand while he carried a small cardboard suitcase with the other.

"I have to leave," he said quietly through his tears. "If I don't, I'll spoil Christmas for everyone."

"But why? And where are you going?" asked Mother.

"I can sleep in my snow fort for a couple of days. I'll come home right after Christmas. I promise."

Mother started to say something about freezing and snow and no mittens or boots, but Daddy, who was not standing just behind her, put his hand on her arm and shook his head. The front door closed, and together they watched from the window as the little figure with the sadly slumped shoulders and no hat trudged across the street and sat down on a snowbank near the corner. It was very dark outside, and cold, and a few snow flurries drifted down on the small boy and his suitcase.

"But he'll freeze!" said Mother.

"Give him a few minutes alone," said Dad quietly. "I think he needs that. Then you can talk to him."

The huddled figure was already dusted with white when Mother walked across the street ten minutes later and sat down beside him on the snowbank.

"What is it, Eric? You've been so good these last

weeks, but I know something's been bothering you since we first started the crib. Can you tell me, honey?"

Ah, Mom . . . don't you see?" he sniffled. "I tried so hard, but I can't do it anymore, and now I'm going to wreck Christmas for everyone." With that he burst into sobs and threw himself into his mother's arms.

"But I don't understand," Mother said, brushing the snow and tears from his face. "What can't you do? And how could you possibly spoil Christmas for us?"

"Mom," the little boy choked, "you just don't know. I got Kelly's name *all four weeks!* And I hate Kelly! I can't do one more nice thing for her or I'll die! I tried, Mom. I really did. I snuck in her room every night and fixed her bed. I even laid out her crummy nightgown. I emptied her wastebasket, and I didn't take a single piece of gum when it was lying right there on her desk. I did some homework for her one night when she was going to the bathroom. Mom, I even let her use my race car one day, but she smashed it right into the wall like always!

"I tried to be nice to her, Mom. Even when she called me a stupid dummy because the crib leg was short, I didn't hit her. And every week, when we picked new names, I thought it would be over. But tonight, when I got her name again, I knew I couldn't

26

do it anymore. I can't do one more nice thing for her, Mom. I just can't! If I try, I'll probably punch her instead. And tomorrow's Christmas Eve. If I stay home and beat up Kelly, I'll spoil Christmas for everybody just when we're ready to put baby Jesus in the crib. Don't you see why I had to leave? Maybe it's not so hard for other people to be nice."

They sat together quietly for a few minutes, Mother's arm around the small boy's shoulders. Only an occasional sniffle and hiccup broke the silence on the snowbank.

Finally, Mother spoke softly. "Eric, I'm so proud of you. Every good thing you did should count double because it was especially hard for you to be nice to Kelly for so long. But you did those good things anyway, one straw at a time. You gave your love when it wasn't easy to give. Maybe that's what the spirit of Christmas is really all about. If it's too easy to give, maybe we're not really giving much of ourselves after all. And maybe it's the *hard* good things and the difficult straws that make that little crib really special.

"You're the one who's probably added the most important straws, and you can be proud of yourself. Now, how would you like a chance to earn a few easy straws like the rest of us? I still have the name I picked tonight in my pocket, and I haven't looked at it yet.

Why don't we switch, just for the last day? It will be our secret."

"That's not cheating?"

"It's not cheating." Mother smiled.

Together they dried the tears, brushed off the snow, and walked back to the house.

The next day the whole family was busy cooking and straightening up the house for Christmas Day, wrapping last-minute presents, and trying hard to keep from bursting with excitement. But even with all the activity and eagerness, a flurry of new straws piled up in the crib, and by nightfall it was almost overflowing. At different times while passing by, each member of the family, big and small, would pause and look at the wonderful pile for a moment, then smile before going on. At last, it was almost time for the tiny crib to be used. But . . . who could really know? One more straw might still make a difference.

For that very reason, just before bedtime, Mother tiptoed quietly to Kelly's room to lay out the little blue nightgown and turn down the bed. But she stopped in the doorway, surprised. Someone had already been there. The nightgown was laid neatly across the bed, and a small red race car rested next to it on the pillow.

The last straw was Eric's after all.

The Jubilee Agreement

TERRY BECK

Unrelieved labor destroys: gradually, but with a deadly certainty, the sledge-hammering of unrelieved stress begins to take its toll, with premature death or disability looming ever larger on the horizon. That is why the Creator ordained Sabbaths . . . and festivals . . . and Jubilees.

Terry Beck, the mother of six children, today lives in Mount Hermon, California. When I asked her about the follow-

ing story's origins, she confided that it was inspired by the Ju-bilees of her own mother.

She offered to participate in this introduction: "My mother was a pioneering woman in many senses of the word . . . The greatest gift I received from observing my parents' marriage is this: that life is enriched by adventure, creativity, and boldness—and strengthened by commitment, support, and the freedom to be unique."

Those who know and love this story have most likely seen only the abridged version. Learning that there was a com-plete text, I persuaded Mrs. Beck to send it to me. Thus, this is probably its first book appearance.

Mama had been out of sorts for weeks. It began when Nathan, the oldest of us children, become involved in the district soccer program. He was the second-grade star of King Richard's Deli. The carpooling, attendance at games, and support meetings ran Mama ragged. Twice a week she loaded four-year-old Jordan, one-year-old Ben, and me, Lydia, six, into the station wagon with Nathan and his teammates, and we'd traipse around the countryside for practices and games. On top of the normal hectic pace of Mama's days, this was, she claimed, heading her straight toward the cuckoo's nest.

It didn't take long before Nathan and I—as self-absorbed as we were—noticed that the energy and enthusiasm Mama normally poured into the small and large things of life were missing. Tiny wrinkles of exhaustion had formed around her startlingly green eyes, and her long auburn hair had lost its bounce and luster. Nathan volunteered to quit the soccer team, but Mama refused to allow it. So, we muddled through the fall, not knowing how to help Mama until the day a wistful suggestion led to a dramatic change in her life and ours.

"Mothers," she declared to my father one evening, "should be rewarded with an occasional vacation all to themselves. A sabbatical or a Jubilee, like they talk about in the Bible. A chance to get away from the urgencies and tedium of everyday life." Her voice lapsed into a deep sigh.

Papa, a giant of a man with dark curly hair and boyish face, walked over to where Mama was folding laundry, sat down on the pile of unmatched socks, and pulled her into his arms.

"Would that help you shake off this confustulation, Beth?" he asked, using one of the conglomerate

33

words from Nathan's toddler days. "Then let's consider this seriously! Take a Jubilee, honey! The children can take care of me for a week." He winked at us behind Mama's back.

Nathan and I knew life would be chaos by the end of one day without Mama. But not wanting to quench the flush of hope that brightened her cheeks, we nodded.

Unwittingly, we'd consented to the Jubilee Agreement. Every three years Mama was to take a week off. She could go wherever she wished, within a stated budget.

Papa encouraged Mama to take her first Jubilee immediately. Mama insisted she needed time to enjoy some anticipation. Besides, she hadn't decided where she wanted to go.

The next month, Mama's spirits soared on a flurry of trips to the library and travel agencies. Soon we were flooded with colorful brochures offering getaways across the country. Mama went into a frenzy of cleaning and cooking, stocking the freezer with a week of dinners. Our neighbor, Evie, agreed to baby-sit while Papa minded his pharmacy.

Papa, Nathan, and I became morose as the departure day drew near. Papa, between his continuing romancing of Mama and obligations at the store, never spent time alone with us. Now he was having second thoughts about the whole Jubilee concept. We older children felt that all of this preparation and fanfare meant that Mama was leaving us for good. Maybe, we plotted, if we were visibly miserable enough, we could get Mama to cancel her plans and stay home.

The scene at the train station on the first day of Jubilee One, as we came to call it, was hysterical. Nathan and I were hysterical with anxiety, Jordan and Ben were hysterical with excitement, and Papa was hysterically perturbed with all of us.

Mama kissed us good-bye with worried eyes.

"Will you really be able to manage?" she asked Papa fearfully. "I had no idea the children would be so upset."

"Go!" our father commanded, pushing the suitcases into the luggage rack. "We are going to be fine. Come along, children!"

To forestall further protests, Papa insisted we play his favorite game: morgue. The rules were simple. Everyone played dead, and the last one to talk, move, or giggle won.

Jordan, the winner of all three rounds, got to open the package Mama left for us on the kitchen table.

Ecstatic "oohs" and "aahs" greeted the two-foot-tall teddy bear pulled from the wrapping. Mama had dressed his soft brown fur in swim trunks and tennis shoes, a reminder that her destination was a health spa just south of the Mexican border.

Tucked under the bear's arm was a card adorned with a blue-gowned angel wearing a cockeyed halo and blowing a slender gold horn. Inside were two messages. On the left:

> My Precious Children,
>
> That I should leave you now, for this Jubilee, is hard, I know. But our separation is only for a short time. This teddy "bears" my promise that, unless an act of God intervenes, I shall come home to you. Talk to the teddy when you miss me and take care of Papa for me.
>
> Love,
> Mama

And on the right:

> Darling John,
>
> I'm hoping this will be a special time for you to get to know our children in a deeper way. Thank you for the gift of Jubilee.

Be assured that neither time nor distance can keep me from loving you with all that I am.

Always,

Beth

Buoyed by the bear (immediately christened "Teddy Talkto" by Jordan) and Mama's love, the week flew by.

The mother who ran from the train into our squealing midst a week later was slimmer, tanner, and more youthful than the one we'd seen off. Her long hair was cut to hang in soft waves around her face, and the smile that had seemed so mechanical when she left was now glorious.

"How I missed you!" she exclaimed repeatedly, hugging us each in turn. She threw herself at Papa, who picked her up and swung her round. While we looked away in embarrassment, they kissed just like in the movies. Yuch!

The pampering massages, sophisticated people, swimming, and horseback riding that Mama gushingly described to us as the highlights of her trip didn't impress us nearly as much as the happiness that radiated from her. By the next week, Mama's frantic schedule hadn't changed, but her outlook had. She went about her daily tasks with a smile and a song.

❖

When Mama returned from Mexico, Teddy Talkto disappeared. Nine months later, as Mama and Papa went to the hospital, he reappeared, dressed in diapers and a tiny T-shirt and snuggling a purple rattle.

Papa phoned us from the hospital that evening to announce Laurel Christina's safe arrival. Ben and Jordan ran straight to Teddy Talkto with the good news. Nathan took the opportunity to explain how Papa, as a former dance class award winner, felt it his duty to claim the first dance of his children's lives. As soon as we were big enough to hold our heads up, Papa ceremoniously waltzed around the house with each baby, humming a little tune and commenting on what fine dancers we were. Nathan demonstrated by picking up Teddy, holding him to his cheek, and dancing solemnly around the room. Entranced, we joined in.

When Mama came home, Teddy Talkto disappeared again, but not thoughts of the dance. Sure enough, the day Laurel began holding her head up steadily, Papa promenaded her through the house, humming softly in her ear. That his older offspring should collapse in a fit of giggles must have mystified him, but Papa continued the dance and didn't probe our secret.

Having survived the first Jubilee, we looked forward to the second. Papa admitted relief that Nathan and I were older and able to help more. With a smile, he reassured Mama not to fear. The Jubilee Agreement did not include a baby within a year of each homecoming.

Mama reached up and patted Papa's chin. "Oh John, what would we do without our Laurel? But don't worry, going away alone makes coming home the best part of the trip. I just hope this trek won't be as hard on me as it was on the early pioneers!"

For Jubilee Two, Mama joined a reenactment of a wagon train crossing the driest stretch of "The Western Trail," forty miles of unrelenting desert in eastern Nevada. The trip was not strictly authentic, she assured us, as the wagons carried ice chests full of food and drink.

Before her car even pulled out of the driveway, we searched the house for Teddy Talkto. We found him mounted on Laurel's rocking horse, dressed as a cowboy sporting a ridiculously huge hat and a red bandanna tied over his nose.

Our week went surprisingly smoothly. As for Mama's week, well, she always described Jubilee Two as a definite "change of pace." The weather was unusually hot and the fleas unusually bad. Bleeding lips and legs blotched with bites were her most visible souvenirs. She told of shivering in her sleeping bag as coyotes howled at the moon, and of striking at a rattlesnake with a shovel one morning as she stepped from the safety of the wagon.

Hardships aside, Jubilee Two had the same magical effect on Mama as Jubilee One. She was again refreshed and renewed in her role as wife and mother. Papa's enthusiasm at her return assured us of their love for each other, and we basked in that security. Could it be, we asked quietly, that while the Jubilee Agreement was meant for Mama, it was good for all of us?

The years passed. Our family took yearly vacations, but it was Mama's Jubilees that defined our lives. During Jubilee we learned not to take her for granted, as well as how to run the washing machine, load the dishwasher, and light the incinerator. We participated vicariously in Mama's travels, and her love of plotting adventure added spice to the daily routine.

Mama spent Jubilee Three at the Seattle World's Fair. We found Teddy Talkto in the shower, hiding under an umbrella and dressed in galoshes and Laurel's outgrown raincoat. We knew what Mama expected from the Pacific Northwest.

By subsisting on the continental breakfast included in the tour package and peanut butter crackers for lunch and dinner, Mama made it to Hawaii for Jubilee Four. Teddy Talkto greeted us on the back lawn, sprawled on a beach towel, wearing a grass skirt and lei.

Jubilee Five and Nathan's freshman year at UCLA were Mama's excuse to "do" Los Angeles. She spent Jubilee Six at a dude ranch in Wyoming and Jubilee Seven at the Grand Canyon.

Papa joined Mama for Jubilee Eight (right after Laurel married). They celebrated this, the end of the Jubilee Agreement, in Acapulco. With all of us wed, there was no one home to see if Mama had dressed Teddy Talkto in a sombrero or mariachi outfit.

Early the next year, Mama began to experience fatigue and stomach pains. Blood tests ordered by the doctor led to exploratory surgery. The final diagnosis of advanced cancer left us devastated. Papa was particularly crushed. He refused to talk about Mama's condition with any of us, and his silence became Mama's biggest concern.

For several months Mama functioned normally, though slowly, and went about putting her affairs in order. She arranged to spend time with each of her children. Laughing time. Crying time. Time to reminisce. Time to express our love.

Papa remained aloof from us all. He waited on Mama like a devoted servant but refused to accept the finality of her illness. Then she was gone, dying with

❖

the same dignity with which she had lived. Even throughout the funeral, with the rest of us weeping noisily around him, Papa was tearless and detached.

The months following Mama's death passed in slow motion. Every joy, every victory seemed muffled without Mama to celebrate with us. Laurel broke through our grief with the birth of her first child, Bethany Jubilee, named for Mama and the agreement that had led to Laurel's own conception. Nathan, Jordan, Ben, and I rejoiced deeply at the news of Bethany's arrival. This new life sparked a joy in us that had been missing for months. Sadly, even holding this enchanting, curly-haired grandchild didn't penetrate the wall of pain wrapping Papa's heart.

Out of our need to heal and continue living, we found excuses to stay away from Papa. His pain was overwhelming, and he held our overtures of comfort and compassion at arm's length. The mention of Mama's name brought a grimace to his once laughing face. We began to fear that we had lost not only the mother we adored but also the father whose encouragement and understanding had girded us throughout our lives.

Hoping to lift Papa out of this depression, we agreed to congregate at the house for a traditional family Christmas that year. Nathan's wife, Melissa, orga-

❖

nized the oldest grandchildren into teams that took turns baking cookies, making fudge, and wrapping gifts. We decorated a magnificent tree with ornaments made through the years, went caroling in the old neighborhood, and attended worship services on Christmas Eve.

By the time Papa went to bed that evening, it was apparent our plan had failed. All of the traditions and treasured memories of Christmas left us aching for Mama. Too discouraged to rally our spirits, we quietly headed for bed.

We adults were in a subdued mood when we gathered the next morning for the grand present-opening. Thank goodness for the boundless enthusiasm of children! Jed, my oldest, played Santa Claus and passed out the gifts.

After the unwrapping and hoopla of the family gifts ended, a large box remained under the tree. There was no tag on it. We asked Papa to open it.

With trembling hands, Papa pulled out the treasured Teddy Talkto. He was dressed as an angel. His flowing blue robe, cockeyed halo, and golden horn matched the attire of the angel on the card he held in his hand. Instantly, Nathan and I recognized the angel. Papa covered his eyes with his hand. Jed opened the card and I nodded for him to read:

"My Precious Children,

"That I should leave you now, for this Jubilee, is hard, I know. But our separation is only for a short time. This teddy "bears" my promise that, unless an act of God intervenes, I shall come home to you. Talk to the teddy when you miss me and take care of Papa for me.

> "Love,
> "Mama"

Jed looked at me questioningly. He had grown up with tales of Teddy Talkto and the Jubilee Agreement, but did not understand the significance of the card. Brushing silent tears from my eyes, I motioned him to continue.

"Darling John,

"I'm hoping this will be a special time for you to get to know our children in a deeper way. Thank you for the gift of Jubilee. Be assured that neither time nor distance can keep me from loving you with all that I am.

> "Always,
> "Beth"

An agonized groan ripped loose from deep within Papa. Tears streaming down his cheeks, he hurried into the kitchen. We looked at each other in silence. Mama! Even in death she reached out to comfort us. It wasn't until one of the small children asked a question about the first Jubilee that we were able to break away from our memories and begin retelling the stories of the Jubilee Agreement and our childhood.

When Papa returned, he carried the tray of cookies and fudge that traditionally followed the opening of presents. Smiling bravely, he faced us and cleared his throat.

"Forgive me," he said with a trembling voice. "Forgive me for trying to deny your mama her final Jubilee." Then, setting down the plate of goodies, he picked up baby Bethany. Humming a little tune, he gingerly waltzed her round the room.

Trouble at the Inn

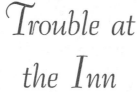

❖

DINA DONOHUE

What could be new about a local nativity play? Children in bathrobes and sheets flubbing their lines. . . . Not always. Sometimes this very spontaneity results in the sudden need to wipe something out of one's eyes.

Stories cannot be judged by length alone, for even though this story is extremely short, so many wrote in, begging that we include it, that we had little choice but to add it to this collection.

For years now whenever Christmas pageants are talked about in a certain little town in the Midwest, someone is sure to mention the name of Wallace Purling. Wally's performance in one annual production of the Nativity play has slipped into the realm of legend. But the old-timers who were in the audience that night never tire of recalling exactly what happened.

Wally was 9 that year and in the second grade, though he should have been in the fourth. Most people in town knew that he had difficulty in keeping up. He was big and clumsy, slow in movement and mind. Still, Wally was well liked by the other children in his class, all of whom were smaller than he, though the boys had trouble hiding their irritation when the uncoordinated Wally would ask to play ball with them.

Most often they'd find a way to keep him off the field, but Wally would hang around anyway—not sulking, just hoping. He was always a helpful boy, a willing and smiling one, and the natural protector, paradoxically, of the underdog. Sometimes if the older boys chased the younger ones away, it would always be Wally who'd say, "Can't they stay? They're no bother."

Wally fancied the idea of being a shepherd with a flute in the Christmas pageant that year, but the play's director, Miss Lumbard, assigned him to a more important role. After all, she reasoned, the Innkeeper did not have too many lines, and Wally's size would make his refusal of lodging to Joseph more forceful.

And so it happened that the usual large, partisan audience gathered for the town's Yuletide extravaganza of the crooks and crèches, of beards, crowns, halos, and a whole stageful of squeaky voices. No one on stage or off was more caught up in the magic of the night than Wallace Purling. They said later that he stood in the wings and watched the performance with such fascination that from time to time Miss Lumbard had to make sure he didn't wander onstage before his cue.

Then the time came when Joseph appeared, slowly, tenderly guiding Mary to the door of the inn. Joseph knocked hard on the wooden door set into the painted backdrop. Wally the Innkeeper was there, waiting.

"What do you want?" Wally said, swinging the door open with a brusque gesture.

"We seek lodging."

49

"Seek it elsewhere." Wally looked straight ahead but spoke vigorously. "The inn is filled."

"Sir, we have asked everywhere in vain. We have traveled far and are very weary."

"There is no room in this inn for you." Wally looked properly stern.

"Please, good innkeeper, this is my wife, Mary. She is heavy with child and needs a place to rest. Surely you must have some small corner for her. She is so tired."

Now for the first time, the Innkeeper relaxed his stiff stance and looked down at Mary. With that, there was a long pause, long enough to make the audience a bit tense with embarrassment.

"No! Begone!" the prompter whispered from the wings.

"No!" Wally repeated automatically. "Begone!"

Joseph sadly placed his arm around Mary, and Mary laid her head upon her husband's shoulder and the two of them started to move away. The Innkeeper did not return inside his inn, however. Wally stood there in the doorway, watching the forlorn couple. His mouth was open, his brow creased with concern, his eyes filling unmistakably with tears.

And suddenly this Christmas pageant became different from all others.

"Don't go, Joseph," Wally called out. "Bring

Mary back." And Wallace Purling's face grew into a bright smile. "You can have *my* room."

Some people in town thought that the pageant had been ruined. Yet there were others—many, many others—who considered it the most Christmas of all Christmas pageants they had ever seen.

The Gold and Ivory Tablecloth

HOWARD C. SCHADE

*If this story were fiction, editors would re-
ject it as being too implausible, too coincidental, to have ever happened. Yet these
storm-induced events did occur, a number
of years after Hitler's armies had ravaged
Europe.*

*Of true stories of Christmas, few are
treasured and reread more than this.*

At Christmastime men and women everywhere gather in their churches to wonder anew at the greatest miracle the world has ever known. But the story I like best to recall was not a miracle—not exactly.

It happened to a pastor who was very young. His church was very old. Once, long ago, it had flourished. Famous men had preached from its pulpit, prayed before its altar. Rich and poor alike had worshiped there and built it beautifully. Now the good days had passed from the section of town where it stood. But the pastor and his young wife believed in their run-down church. They felt that with paint, hammer, and faith they could get it in shape. Together they went to work.

But late in December a severe storm whipped through the river valley, and the worst blow fell on the little church—a huge chunk of rain-soaked plaster fell out of the inside wall just behind the altar. Sorrowfully the pastor and his wife swept away the mess, but they couldn't hide the ragged hole.

The pastor looked at it and had to remind himself quickly, "Thy will be done!" But his wife wept, "Christmas is only two days away!"

That afternoon the dispirited couple attended the auction held for the benefit of a youth group. The auctioneer opened a box and shook out of its folds a handsome gold-and-ivory lace tablecloth. It was a magnificent item, nearly 15 feet long. But it, too, dated from a long-vanished era. Who, today, had any use for such a thing? There were a few half-hearted bids. Then the pastor was seized with what he thought was a great idea. He bid it in for $6.50.

He carried the cloth back to the church and tacked it up on the wall behind the altar. It completely hid the hole! And the extraordinary beauty of its shimmering handwork cast a fine, holiday glow over the chancel. It was a great triumph. Happily he went back to preparing his Christmas sermon.

Just before noon on the day of Christmas Eve, as the pastor was opening the church, he noticed a woman standing in the cold at the bus stop.

"The bus won't be here for 40 minutes!" he called, and invited her into the church to get warm.

She told him that she had come from the city that morning to be interviewed for a job as governess to the children of one of the wealthy families in town but she had been turned down. A war refugee, her English was imperfect.

The woman sat down in a pew and chafed her hands and rested. After a while she dropped her head and prayed. She looked up as the pastor began to adjust the great gold-and-ivory lace cloth across the hole. She rose suddenly and walked up the steps of the chancel.

She looked at the tablecloth. The pastor smiled and started to tell her about the storm damage, but she didn't seem to listen. She took up a fold of the cloth and rubbed it between her fingers.

"It is mine!" she said. "It is my banquet cloth!" She lifted up a corner and showed the surprised pastor that there were initials monogrammed on it. "My husband had the cloth made especially for me in Brussels! There could not be another like it."

For the next few minutes the woman and the pastor talked excitedly together. She explained that she was Viennese; that she and her husband had opposed the Nazis and decided to leave the country. They were advised to go separately. Her husband put her on a train for Switzerland. They planned that he would join her as soon as he could arrange to ship their household goods across the border.

She never saw him again. Later she heard that he had died in a concentration camp.

"I have always felt that it was my fault—to leave without him," she said. "Perhaps these years of wandering have been my punishment!"

The pastor tried to comfort her, urged her to take the cloth with her. She refused. Then she went away.

As the church began to fill on Christmas Eve, it was clear that the cloth was going to be a great success. It had been skillfully designed to look its best by candlelight.

After the service, the pastor stood at the doorway; many people told him that the church looked beautiful. One gentle-faced, middle-aged man—he was the local clock-and-watch repairman—looked rather puzzled.

"It is strange," he said in his soft accent. "Many years ago my wife—God rest her—and I owned such a cloth. In our home in Vienna, my wife put it on the table"—and here he smiled—"only when the bishop came to dinner!"

The pastor suddenly became very excited. He told the jeweler about the woman who had been in church earlier in the day.

The startled jeweler clutched the pastor's arm. "Can it be? Does she live?"

Together the two got in touch with the family who had interviewed her. Then, in the pastor's car they started for the city. And as Christmas Day was born, this man and his wife—who had been separated through so many saddened Yuletides—were reunited.

To all who heard this story, the joyful purpose of the storm that had knocked a hole in the wall of the church was now quite clear. Of course, people said it was a miracle, but I think you will agree it was the season for it!

A Father for Christmas

AUTHOR UNKNOWN

Better than any other tale I know, this old story hammers home a great truth: the line of demarcation between success and failure in life is paper thin, as thin as the line between happiness and tragedy. Quite often the difference is nothing more than a kind heart and a realization that each of us is our brother's keeper.

Sheriff John Charles Olsen let out a sigh so hefty it blew an apple core clear off his desk. There'd been times in his life when he'd felt worse. The night he'd spent in the swamp behind the Sundquist place with a broken leg and about a million mosquitoes for company was one such time. But there'd never been a time when he'd wanted less to be a sheriff.

"Are you deaf?" Mart Dahlberg demanded.

Sheriff Olsen looked across at where his deputy was typing out letters in his usual neat and fast way. "Did you say something?"

"Only three times. Didn't you promise the fellow you'd be out there by noon?"

"It ain't noon yet."

"It will be by the time you get there."

Sheriff Olsen hauled himself, slow and heavy, to his feet.

"Sure you don't want me to go along?" Mart asked, and his voice was gentler sounding.

The sheriff shook his head. "No, not much stuff out there. Just four chairs and a table and the kids' clothes and some bedding."

"Well, I wish you'd get started," Mart said. "You got to be back here and into your Santa Claus outfit by three, remember."

"I haven't forgotten," the sheriff answered. He sounded snappish, but he couldn't help it.

Mart got up from his desk. "Look, John," he said, "take it easy. Folks get evicted from their homes all the time."

"Not a week before Christmas, they don't," the sheriff growled.

He slammed shut the office door and went out of the courthouse to where his car was parked. He gave a quick look at how the trailer was fastened, then he got into the car and slammed that door shut, too.

Maybe it wasn't anybody's fault what had happened. But it made the sheriff feel awfully queer in his stomach to have to move three little kids out of their home just before he was going to dress up in a Santa Claus outfit and hand out gifts to other kids at the annual Christmas celebration!

Sheriff Olsen started up the engine and turned on the heater. Then he turned it off and wiped the sweat off his forehead with his mitten. Likely a man with more brains than the sheriff had could have fixed things right for Stephen Reade.

Sam Merske called Stephen Reade a deadbeat and a phony, but that was because Reade hadn't made a good tenant farmer. Two years ago, when Reade had rented the farm from Merske, Merske had called Reade a fine, upstanding personality.

Sheriff Olsen had argued for months with Merske about Reade and the kids, figuring that all Reade needed was another summer to get things going right. But Sam Merske was a businessman and he expected his farm to produce and make money for him. Finally he'd taken Reade to court.

After that, the sheriff had done his arguing with Judge Martinson, but the judge said that Sam Merske had been very generous and patient with Reade, and that it was understandable Sam's wanting to get a competent man settled on his farm before spring came.

"This man, Reade," the judge had said, "is obviously not fitted to farm. That has been proven to my satisfaction, not only by his inability to make his rent payments but also by the condition the county agent tells me the farm is in. Let us not fog our judgment, John, with undue sentimentality. It will be far better for both Reade and his children if we face the issue squarely."

It wasn't Stephen Reade's fault what had happened. You have to be kind of raised to it to know what to do when your cow takes sick or the weather mildews your raspberries. All his life since he was a kid, Reade had been in the selling business in New York City, going from door to door, first with magazine sub-

64

scriptions, and then with stockings, and finally with vacuum cleaners. It took hard work and brains and a lot more courage than the sheriff himself had to go around ringing doorbells and asking strange women to buy things from you. But Stephen Reade had sold enough to support a wife and three children.

After the third child was born, Mrs. Reade had been sick all the time. She'd been raised on a farm in Oregon, and she figured living in a big city was what made her sick. So when she knew she wasn't going to live, she'd made her husband promise he'd take the kids to the country.

Reade had promised faithfully, and after his wife was gone he'd taken what was left of their savings and headed for Oregon. He'd gone as far as the bus depot in St. Paul when he'd read an ad. The ad had said that anyone with initiative and enterprise wanting to rent an A-one farm should apply to Sam Merske, proprietor of the Merske Dry Goods Store in Minnewashta County.

Sam had demanded three months' rent in advance, and that was all he'd ever gotten out of Reade. The cow and the chickens had taken all the leftover cash that Reade had, and the cow hadn't lived very long.

Johanna Olsen, the sheriff's wife, had bought all her eggs off of Reade for two months. After that, for

❖

another two months she'd bought as many as Reade had to sell. And, after that, there weren't enough hens left to give the Reade youngsters an egg each for their breakfasts.

The plan was to move the Reade family into the two empty rooms above the Hovander Grain and Feed Store. It wasn't a permanent arrangement, because Hovander didn't like the idea. "Eight days is all they can stay. I ain't no charitable institution, and I wouldn't do the favor for nobody but you, John."

But the eight days would get the Reade kids through Christmas.

Sheriff Olsen brought the car and the trailer up along-side the farmhouse. There was a big railed-in porch running around three sides of the house and you could see how a widower with three children would have liked the looks of the porch the minute he saw it—forgetting how hard a big old house was to heat.

The sheriff knocked at the door. After a minute he heard someone running and then Ellen's voice said, "Robbie, don't go near that door; I'm supposed to answer." In another minute, the door opened a crack.

Sheriff Olsen said, " 'Lo, Ellen."

Ellen said, "Hello, Mr. Olsen," but she didn't

smile back. "My father's out for the present, but you're welcome to wait in the kitchen. It's warmest there."

Sheriff Olsen sat down on one of the four chairs pulled up to a card table. On the table was a bundle tied up in a blanket; near the back door was a barrel covered with newspapers, and three suitcases fastened with ropes.

The sheriff said, "You sure been busy."

"I helped with everything," Robbie said.

Ellen said, "The stove belongs to Mr. Merske, and so do the beds and the clock. But the chairs and the table are all paid for and so they belong to us."

Sheriff Olsen looked at the clock. "Did your pa say when he'd be back?"

"He's gone for something," Ellen said.

Robbie said, "Dad's gone to get us a surprise. Letty thinks he's buying her a doll, but Dad said what he's getting for us is heaps more important than anything you can buy in a store."

Sheriff Olsen smiled at Letty and she came over and put her head down on his knee. She was about 4 and she wasn't worried yet about how things were in the world.

When it got to be about half past 12, the sheriff said, "Maybe we should all drive down the road a ways and give a lift to your pa!"

Ellen slid down from the window sill. "Are you getting restless, Mr. Olsen?" she asked.

67

"Kinda."

"Well, when you get awful restless, I'm supposed to give you a letter." She started toward the parlor door. Then she turned. "But first, you have to be awful restless."

"I am awful restless," he answered with a worried look on his kind face.

In half a minute, she was back with an envelope. Inside was a sheet of paper that had been written on with pencil:

"To the Sheriff of Minnewashta County: I, Stephen Reade, being of sound mind and body, do herewith declare that I relinquish all legal claim to my three children, Ellen, Robert, and Letitia Reade. I do this as my Christmas gift to them, so that they may be legally adopted by some family that will take care of them. I herewith swear never to make myself known to their new parents. They are good children and will make their new parents happy.

Yours very truly,

Your grateful friend, Stephen Reade."

"Does it tell about my doll?" Letty asked, jumping up and down.

"Does my father say when he'll be back, Mr.

Olsen?" Ellen asked. She was standing very straight at the sink, making little pleats in her dress. "Does he?"

Sheriff Olsen looked at the clock, and then at his watch. There'd be a freight train pulling out of the station in 38 minutes, and if Reade hadn't hitched a ride on a truck, he'd be waiting to bum one on the freight. But you couldn't chase after a deserting father with the fellow's kids in the back of your car.

"Does he?" Ellen asked again.

Sheriff Olsen gave a big hearty smile. "Well, what do you know about that? Your dad's changed his plans. He wants you should stay the afternoon with my wife. So, quick now, put on your coats and caps and boots while I unhitch the trailer."

"But aren't we taking our chairs and things, Mr. Olsen," Ellen asked.

"I'll come back for 'em later. Where's your boots, Letty?"

"Mr. Olsen, I don't think my father would want us to leave without taking our furniture with us."

"Look, my wife's going to take you to the Christmas celebration and you'll get presents from Santa Claus and everything. Only we gotta hurry, see?"

"Daddy's getting me a present," Letty said.

Robbie shouted, "I think we'd better wait here for Daddy."

"There'll be a Christmas tree," the sheriff said, "and hot cocoa to drink and peanut butter sandwiches. Robbie, you got brains, see if you can find Letty's mittens. I got her boots here."

Next Ellen spoke up: "We aren't supposed to go to the Christmas celebration, Mr. Olsen. My father told us it's just for the children who live in town."

"Well, that's the big surprise your pa's got for you. Santa Claus wants the three Reade kids to be special guests. Letty, stick your thumb in the hole that was meant for your thumb in this mitten."

"I want my daddy," Letty squealed. "I want my daddy to take me to see Santa Claus."

"She's scared because Daddy isn't here," Robbie said. "Aren't you scared 'cause Daddy isn't here, Letty?"

Sheriff Olsen grabbed hold of Letty. "How good can you ride piggyback?" With that, he rushed her off to the car.

Going over the slippery road with the three children, the sheriff had to drive slowly and carefully back into town. Right away, when the sheriff honked, Johanna came running out of the house.

"Johanna, they haven't eaten yet. And could you please phone down to the Christmas committee and tell them that you're bringing three extra children so they will have time to get their gifts wrapped right."

Johanna opened the back door to the car, and the three Reade youngsters moved out toward the smile she gave them like they were three new-hatched chicks heading for the feel of something warm.

"Wow!" said Johanna. "Am I ever lucky! There's a whole big chocolate cake in the kitchen, and me worrying who was going to help to frost and eat it."

With the kids out of the car, the sheriff drove kind of crazy. Once he was past the courthouse and heading for the station, the traffic thinned out and there wasn't anybody's neck to worry about except his own.

The freight was in, and the sheriff drove straight up onto the platform. Lindahl, who was stationmaster, gave a yelp, but when he saw it was the sheriff, he yelled, "What's he look like?" and started running down the length of the train.

Sheriff Olsen headed east toward the engine, and found where somebody had once been crouching down in the snow on the embankment.

It was an open boxcar, and likely Reade had seen the sheriff already, but the sheriff called out Reade's name anyhow. Then he pulled himself up into the car.

It took half a minute for the sheriff to get used to the half light, but all that time Stephen Reade didn't move or try to get past him through the door. He just sat huddled up in his corner, pretending like he wasn't there.

71

❖

Sheriff Olsen went over to him and put his hands under Reade's elbows and pulled him to his feet. Reade didn't say anything when the sheriff shoved him down off the boxcar into the snow. But when they were in the sheriff's car, the train gave a whistle and Reade said, in a whisper, "I was close to making it."

The sheriff drove around behind where the Ladies' Shakespeare Study Society had put a row of evergreens. He kept the heater going, and after a couple of minutes Stephen Reade stopped shaking some. The sheriff got out the vacuum bottle and poured coffee into its cap.

All of a sudden Reade gave a groan. "Let me out of here! For their sake, you've got to let me get away!" He started to rock back and forth, with his hands holding tight to his knees. "You've got to believe me! I'm no good for those kids! I've lost my nerve. I'm frightened. I'm frightened sick!"

For a long time the sheriff just sat next to Stephen Reade, wanting one minute to break the guy's neck for him, and the next minute to put his arm around him, and not knowing any of the time what was right to do.

After a couple of minutes he said, "A while back, you claimed I didn't know what it was like to be scared. Well, sometimes I get scared, too. Take like this

72

afternoon. This afternoon I got to dress up crazy and hand out presents to a whole roomful of kids. Last night I didn't sleep so good either, worrying about it."

Stephen Reade snorted.

"Well, it ain't easy like maybe you think," Sheriff John went on. "I have to get up on a platform, and all the kids'll be staring at me, and sometimes their folks come too."

"You certainly make it sound tragic."

"OK, if you don't figure it's so hard, you do it. I'll make a bargain with you. You be Santa Claus for me, and I'll find you a job. And while you're doing a good turn for both me and yourself, Ellen and Robbie and Letty will sure get a kick out of seeing their pa acting Santa Claus to all the kids in town."

For a long time Reade just sat staring through the windshield. Then he said, with his voice low and sober, "You couldn't find me a job. There isn't a man in the whole county who'd be half-wit enough to hire the loony that made hash out of Merske's farm. And you know it." Then he faced around to the sheriff. "But I'll play at being Santa Claus if you want me to. I've been owing you some sort of thanks for a couple of years."

Ten minutes later, the sheriff had Stephen Reade

73

❖

holed up in the washroom opposite his office. He pointed out where the outfit was hanging in the corner. "You better put the whiskers and cap on, too, while you got a mirror," he said. "I'll keep watch outside."

Sheriff Olsen closed the washroom door and stepped back almost into his deputy's arms.

"What you got in there?" Mart Dahlberg said.

"Stephen Reade. He's going to be Santa Claus."

"You crazy or something?" Mart asked. "You've been Santa Claus for five years. What you want to go and give your part to that dope for?"

"Look, Mart, don't yell. Reade's feeling awful low, see? Getting evicted and not having a job or nothing. And I kinda figured handing out the presents to all the kids would maybe pep him up some."

"The committee won't let him."

"The committee won't know until it's too late," the sheriff explained. "Maybe I figured crazy, but I had to figure something. And, anyhow, he promised his kids a good surprise."

Mart gave a gentle pat on the sheriff's back. "Well," he said, "I can pray for you, but I don't figure it will help much."

Twenty minutes later, Sheriff Olsen poked his head into the kitchen behind the church's big recreation room.

Mrs. Bengtson looked around from washing cocoa cups. "The eating's done with, John," she said. "And they're singing carols while they wait for you."

Sheriff Olsen said, "Thanks." He motioned Stephen Reade to slip past through the kitchen to the door that opened out on the little stage. Then he moved himself, quiet and unnoticed, around to the back of the recreation room.

The piano was playing "Silent Night" and the place was jam-packed. The sheriff took off his hat and wiped his face. Then he sat down at the end of the bench that held Johanna and the three Reade kids. He smiled across the heads of the three kids at Johanna, and then he closed his hand over the hot paw that little Ellen had wriggled onto his knee.

Up on the stage the tree was a beautiful sight. It was nine feet tall, and the committee had decorated it with pretty balls, lights, and popcorn chains. Under the tree were the presents. The wrapping paper had all come from Merske's Dry Goods Store because this year Sam Merske was chairman of the committee and most of the presents had been bought at his store. Some of the paper was white and had green bells on it and some was red with white bells, and each bell had printed on it one of the letters of M E R S K E. And they were a beautiful sight, too. But sitting next to the presents, low under the tree, hunched up like a discouraged rabbit, was Santa Claus.

Sheriff Olsen flattened his hat out on his knee. Mart had been right. Wearing a beard on his chin and putting stuffing over his stomach weren't going to put pep into Stephen Reade. All they were going to do was spoil the show for the children and make Reade feel more miserable even than before! Then the music stopped and the sheriff folded his hat in two. Mart had said he would pray and maybe he wasn't forgetting to.

All of a sudden a little kid down front squealed, "Merry Christmas, Santa Claus!" And after that, the whole room was full of loving squeals and chirpings and calls of "Hi, Santa!"

Stephen Reade straightened up his shoulders a bit and then he reached out a hand for one of the packages. Sheriff Olsen began to feel some better. At least, Reade was remembering what he was up on the stage for, and maybe the kids wouldn't notice that Santa Claus didn't have his whole heart in the business.

Then a voice said, hoarse and angry, "Move over," and Sam Merske plunked himself down at the end of the bench.

76

Sheriff Olsen gave a low groan, and Merske said, "Surprised to see me, huh?"

"Kinda," the sheriff muttered.

"You got the nerve to be sitting here," Merske said. "Who you got up there behind those whiskers?"

Sheriff Olsen wet his lips and then he opened his mouth, figuring to say it was a friend. But Ellen Reade was quicker at opening hers. Ellen leaned over the sheriff's knees and lifted her face up, eager and excited.

"It's my father, Mr. Merske," she whispered. "Isn't he *wonderful?*" Then she gave a sigh like she was stuffed full of a good dinner, and turned back to stare at the stage again.

Sheriff Olsen stared at the stage too, but the tree and Santa Claus and the little boy who was getting his present were all blurred together because of the awful way the sheriff was feeling.

Sam Merske said, "So you put Stephen Reade up there in the whiskers and clothes and things that I supplied. Ain't that just beautiful?"

On the stage, a little girl was getting her package, and being a little girl, was remembering to say "Thank you."

Sam Merske said, "I'll get you for this. Putting a dead beat up there to hand out stuff that's wrapped with my paper and tied with my string! A no-good loafer that'll ruin the whole show! A no-good——"

His voice was getting louder, and the sheriff stuck his elbow hard into Sam Merske's ribs to make him shut up before the Reade kids could hear what he was saying.

But just shutting him up for now wasn't going to help. There were an awful lot of ways Merske could shame Stephen Reade in front of his children——like taking away the table and chairs that Ellen had counted on belonging to her family.

Sheriff Olsen tried to swallow, but his mouth was too dry. His throat was dry the same as his mouth. But his face and neck were so wet it would have taken a couple of bath towels to mop them.

It wasn't just a dumb thing the sheriff had gone and done; it was a plain crazy thing.

"Look, Sam," the sheriff whispered, "I gotta talk with you outside."

"Not with me," Merske said. "I'm sitting right here until I can lay my hands personal on that bum."

"Crazy" was what his deputy had called the sheriff's scheme. But Mart Dahlberg had been kind and generous. "Wicked" was the word he ought to have used.

And then all of a sudden a little boy began to yowl.

"It's Johnny Pilshek," Ellen said. "He's mad 'cause Louie Horbetz got a cowboy hat and all he got was mittens."

Every year it happened like that. Two or maybe three or four kids would complain about their presents, and that was why the committee always hid half a dozen boxes of something such as crayons under the sheet to give them. But Stephen Reade didn't know about the extras, because the sheriff had forgotten to tell him.

Johnny Pilshek marched back up on the stage. He stuck out his lower lip and shoved the mittens at Santa Claus. "I don't want mittens," Johnny howled. "Mittens aren't a real present."

Santa Claus took the mittens and inspected them. "Most mittens aren't a real present," he said, "but these mittens are something special. They're made of interwoven, reprocessed wool, Johnny. That's what the label says. And we had to order them especially for you at the North Pole, Johnny! Everywhere, boys have been asking me to bring them this special kind of mitten, but we haven't been able to supply the demand."

"I've got mittens already," Johnny muttered. "I don't want no more."

Santa reached out and took one of Johnny's hands and inspected it careful as he had the mittens.

"Certainly you've got mittens already, Johnny.

But they aren't like these. Do you know why we had these made for you, Johnny? We had these made for you because your hands are rather special. You've got to keep those fingers of yours supple, Johnny. A baseball player, when he's your age, gets his fingers stiff from the cold, and what happens? He winds up in the minor leagues, that's what happens."

He put the mittens back into Johnny's hand. "And we don't want you in anything except the major teams, Johnny."

"Gee," said Johnny. Then he turned around and walked down off the platform, flexing the fingers of his right hand, slow and thoughtful all the way.

Sheriff Olsen let out the breath he'd been holding; he could see now how Stephen Reade had made a living for his wife and kids out of going from door to door with magazines and hosiery and vacuum cleaners. The sheriff looked down at Ellen, and Ellen looked up at the sheriff and gave a big smile.

"He sure *is* wonderful!" the sheriff whispered to her.

And then a little girl sitting next to Johnny Pilshek stood up and asked, solemn and polite, if she could bring her present back too. She'd wrapped it up in the paper again, and she kept it hidden behind her until she was up on the stage.

"I think it's a mistake," she said in an unhappy kind of a whisper. "What I got wasn't meant for a girl."

Santa took the package. "We don't often make a mistake, April," he told her, "but let's see." He opened the package up on his knees.

"I don't mind it's being a muffler," April said, "but that one's meant for a boy. I know, because it's just like one they've got in Mr. Merske's store in the boy's section for 69 cents. And it's not one bit pretty, either."

Stephen Reade held up the heavy gray scarf. "You're right, April," he said. "This was made for a boy and it's not one bit pretty. All the same, we chose it for you. And here's the reason why. It was chosen especially to protect your voice."

"I don't care. I don't want to wear it."

"You're pretty, April, and someday you'll be even prettier. But this is a fact. To get into the movies or on TV you've got to have a pretty face, but you've got to have something else too. You've got to have a pretty voice, one that's been properly protected by"—he turned over one corner of the scarf—"by 40 percent wool, 60 percent cotton, vat-dyed."

He draped the thing over April's arm, and after a little bit, April began to stroke it.

"Should I wear it all the time, Santa?"

"No. Just when the temperature's below freezing, April. Have your mother check the thermometer every time you go out, and when it's below 32, then you wear it."

"Yes, sir—I mean, yes, thank you, Santa Claus."

Five minutes later, the lady who played the piano sat down again and started in on "Hark the Herald Angels Sing." On the stage Stephen Reade was standing up, singing, and motioning with his arms for everybody to join in. But the sheriff couldn't join in. He couldn't even open his mouth, let alone get any singing out.

Stephen Reade had done what the sheriff had asked him to, and he'd made a good job of it. And in return the sheriff had got Reade and his kids in a worse fix than ever.

The sheriff turned and looked at Sam Merske. He wasn't singing either—just scowling and muttering to himself.

The sheriff wet his lips. "Sam," he said.

Merske turned and glared. "So that was the gag," he said. "Pretty slick, pretty slick, arranging for him to give me a personal demonstration of his selling ability. Pretty slick."

"Huh?" said the sheriff, and when the song ended and the next one hadn't yet begun, he said, "Huh?" again.

"OK," said Merske, "you win this time. He gets the job."

"What do you mean?" the sheriff asked slow and careful. "You mean you're fixing to give Stephen Reade a job in your store?"

"With the competition I've got from the mail orders, I'd give a shoplifter a job if he could sell like that guy can. He may not be a farmer, but he's a real salesman." Then he scratched at the top of his head and glared some more at the sheriff. "What gets me is that I never put you down for having either the brains or the brass to swing a deal like that. How'd you hit on it?"

Sheriff Olsen didn't answer. It would take an awful lot of talking to explain to Merske how sometimes things worked out fine even without any brains to help you. And, besides, the piano was getting started on "Jingle Bells," which was a tune the sheriff knew extra well.

Sheriff Olsen opened his mouth wide. He could tell from the way the folks in front turned around to frown at him that he was drowning them out. But he didn't care. There wasn't any better time than a week before Christmas, he figured, for bursting out loud and merry . . .

A Gift from
the Heart

NORMAN VINCENT
PEALE

What do you give to someone who already has everything money can buy? In our affluent society, this is anything but an uncommon question.

Norman Vincent Peale, so recently laid to rest, was for most of this past century one of the most beloved——and certainly most read——preachers in America. As pastor of New York's prestigious Marble Collegiate Church, he gained a national following. Later, he became the guiding *spirit of one of the most cherished inspirational magazines we have,* Guideposts.

But out of all his vast output, nothing is reread with more frequency——or tears——than this brief true story.

New York City, where I live, is impressive at any time, but as Christmas approaches, it's overwhelming. Store windows blaze with light and color, furs and jewels. Golden angels, 40 feet tall, hover over Fifth Avenue. Wealth, power, opulence . . . nothing in the world can match this fabulous display.

Through the gleaming canyons, people hurry to find last-minute gifts. Money seems to be no problem. If there's a problem, it's that the recipients so often have everything they need or want that it's hard to find anything suitable, anything that will really say "I love you."

Last December, as Christ's birthday drew near, a stranger was faced with just that problem. She had come from Switzerland to live in an American home and perfect her English. In return, she was willing to act as secretary, mind the grandchildren, do anything

86

she was asked. She was just a girl in her late teens. Her name was Ursula.

One of the tasks her employers gave Ursula was keeping track of Christmas presents as they arrived. There were many, and all would require acknowledgment. Ursula kept a faithful record, but with a growing sense of concern. She was grateful to her American friends; she wanted to show her gratitude by giving them a Christmas present. But nothing that she could buy with her small allowance could compare with the gifts she was recording daily. Besides, even without these gifts, it seemed to her that her employers already had everything.

At night, from her window, Ursula could see the snowy expanse of Central Park, and beyond it the jagged skyline of the city. Far below, in the restless streets, taxis hooted and traffic lights winked red and green. It was so different from the silent majesty of the Alps that at times she had to blink back tears of the homesickness she was careful never to show. It was in the solitude of her little room, a few days before Christmas, that her secret idea came to Ursula.

It was almost as if a voice spoke clearly, inside her head. "It's true," said the voice, "that many people in this city have much more than you do. But surely there are many who have far less. If you will think about this, you may find a solution to what's troubling you."

Ursula thought long and hard. Finally on her day off, which was Christmas Eve, she went to a great department store. She moved slowly along the crowded aisles, selecting and rejecting things in her mind. At last she bought something, and had it wrapped in gaily colored paper. She went out into the gray twilight and looked helplessly around. Finally, she went up to a doorman, resplendent in blue and gold. "Excuse, please," she said in her hesitant English, "can you tell me where to find a poor street?"

"A poor street, miss?" said the puzzled man.

"Yes, a very poor street. The poorest in the city."

The doorman looked doubtful. "Well, you might try Harlem. Or down in the Village. Or the Lower East Side, maybe."

But these names meant nothing to Ursula. She thanked the doorman and walked along, threading her way through the stream of shoppers until she came to a tall policeman. "Please," she said, "can you direct me to a very poor street in . . . in Harlem?"

The policeman looked at her sharply and shook his head. "Harlem's no place for you, miss." And he blew his whistle and sent the traffic swirling past.

Holding her package carefully, Ursula walked on, head bowed against the sharp wind. If a street looked poorer than the one she was on, she took it. But none seemed like the slums she had heard about. Once she stopped a woman, "Please, where do the very poor people live?" But the woman gave her a stare and hurried on.

Darkness came sifting from the sky. Ursula was cold and discouraged and afraid of becoming lost. She came to an intersection and stood forlornly on the corner. What she was trying to do suddenly seemed foolish, impulsive, absurd. Then, through the traffic's roar, she heard the cheerful tinkle of a bell. On the corner opposite, a Salvation Army man was making his traditional Christmas appeal.

At once Ursula felt better; the Salvation Army was a part of life in Switzerland, too. Surely this man could tell her what she wanted to know. She waited for the light, then crossed over to him. "Can you help me? I'm looking for a baby. I have here a little present for the poorest baby I can find." And she held up the package with the green ribbon and the gaily colored paper.

Dressed in gloves and overcoat a size too big for him, he seemed a very ordinary man. But behind his steel-rimmed glasses his eyes were kind. He looked at Ursula and stopped ringing his bell. "What sort of present?" he asked.

"A little dress. For a small, poor baby. Do you know of one?"

"Oh, yes," he said. "Of more than one, I'm afraid."

"Is it far away? I could take a taxi, maybe?"

The Salvation Army man wrinkled his forehead. Finally he said, "It's almost six o'clock. My relief will show up then. If you want to wait, and if you can afford a dollar taxi ride, I'll take you to a family in my own neighborhood who needs just about everything."

"And they have a small baby?"

"A very small baby."

"Then," said Ursula joyfully, "I wait!"

The substitute bell-ringer came. A cruising taxi slowed. In its welcome warmth, she told her new friend about herself, how she came to be in New York, what she was trying to do. He listened in silence, and the taxi driver listened too. When they reached their destination, the driver said, "Take your time, miss. I'll wait for you."

On the sidewalk, Ursula stared up at the forbidding tenement—dark, decaying, saturated with hopelessness. A gust of wind, iron-cold, stirred the refuse in the street and rattled the reeling ashcans. "They live on the third floor," the Salvation Army man said. "Shall we go up?"

But Ursula shook her head. "They would try to thank me, and this is not from me." She pressed the package into his hand. "Take it up for me, please. Say it's from . . . from someone who has everything."

The taxi bore her swiftly from dark streets to lighted ones, from misery to abundance. She tried to visualize the Salvation Army man climbing the stairs, the knock, the explanation, the package being opened, the dress on the baby. It was hard to do.

Arriving at the apartment house on Fifth Avenue where she lived, she fumbled in her purse. But the driver flicked the flag up. "No charge, miss."

"No charge?" echoed Ursula, bewildered.

"Don't worry," the driver said. "I've been paid." He smiled at her and drove away.

Ursula was up early the next day. She set the table with special care. By the time she had finished, the family was awake, and there was all the excitement and laughter of Christmas morning. Soon the living room was a sea of gay discarded wrappings. Ursula thanked everyone for the presents she received. Finally, when there was a lull, she began to explain hesitantly why there seemed to be none from her. She told about going to the department store. She told about the Salvation Army man. She told about the taxi driver. When she finished, there was a long silence. No one seemed to trust himself to speak. "So you see," said Ursula, "I try to do a kindness in your name. And this is my Christmas present to you . . ."

How do I happen to know all this? I know it because ours was the home where Ursula lived. Ours was the Christmas she shared. We were like many Americans, so richly blessed that to this child from across the sea there seemed to be nothing she could add to the material things we already had. And so she offered something of far greater value: a gift from the heart, an act of kindness carried out in our name.

Strange, isn't it? A shy Swiss girl, alone in a great impersonal city. You would think that nothing she could do would affect anyone. And yet, by trying to give away love, she brought the true spirit of Christmas into our lives, the spirit of selfless giving. That was Ursula's secret—and she shared it with us all.

Christmas in the New World

ROSINA KIEHLBAUCH

The year was 1874 and the Dakota prairies were lonely, cold, and virtually treeless. How was a German immigrant family, transplanted from the steppes of Russia only three months before, supposed to find a Christmas where not even a Lutheran church had been constructed?

Where would a tree come from? Where, for that matter, would toys, gifts? This was the dilemma that faced Johannes and Codray (Katherina), but they set about making the best of it.

Unique in Christmas literature is Rosina Kiehlbauch's trilogy of three Christmases (1874, 1884, 1894) on the Dakota frontier. Nothing I have ever read is comparable to these three accounts: not only do they have power and pathos, but they also graphically reveal the interweaving changes in frontier life.

Rosina Kiehlbauch's daughter, Catherine Sherry, felt so strongly that these memories deserved a wider audience that she made them available to the editors of The American Historical Society of Germans from Russia in Lincoln, Nebraska, who ran them in three issues of their Journal.

The institutions of the dreaded Pelznickel and beloved Kristkindle were born in the Valley of the Rhine, and shadowed by the alpine heights where Germany, France, and Switzerland meet. When those native to this region emigrated to America, they brought these Christmas traditions with them.

We begin with the earliest of the three accounts.

❖ ❖ ❖

Eighteen hundred and seventy-four. In a sod house on the Dakota prairie, 6,000 miles from last Christmas in

Russia, Johannes and Codray Kulbach were facing the holiday season with many misgivings.

Since September, when they took up their Clear Lake homestead, these south Russian German immigrants had been so busy putting up a sod house in which to live and sod shelters for their farm animals and plowing fields that the trip to Yankton for holiday supplies and a few extra comforts for the long winter had been repeatedly postponed.

What would they do about Christmas for their three little children? The demands of homesteading left no time for the pioneer parents to provide more than the bare necessities for pioneer life. There was still money in the black lacquer cash box. It had provided first class passage on the S.S. *Brunswick* from the old country. In the new country they had bought farm implements, a team of horses, and the necessary household furnishings. It wasn't the lack of money; it was the lack of time now that snow had come so early and the menace of a Dakota blizzard that made the two-day trip to town hazardous even with good horses.

During the weeks spent on the seemingly barren prairie, the immigrants had learned to solve all kinds of problems. Surely somehow they would also solve the problem of a tree and gifts for the children's first Christmas in the land of their adoption. Was it not for the children's sake that they had left their comfortable home in south Russia and come to America? They must not fail in this their first Christmas celebration.

Johannes and his wife were courageous pioneers, descendants of liberty-loving Swabians, who almost a century earlier, rather than submit to compulsory military service in Württemberg, had immigrated to the wild steppes of south Russia and there, under the direct protection of the Russian Crown, had built their homes, tilled the soil, and kept the holy days of the Lutheran Church with appropriate celebrations. Surely God was a God of the prairies as well as of the steppes, and if He marked the sparrow's fall He would also mark the little soddie so trustfully launched on the prairie's endless sea of grass.

In the land of the Dakotas there was no cathedral with its familiar Advent services to remind old and young that the holidays were drawing near. The Church Almanac in which the homesteaders checked each day (there was no other way of keeping track of the days) showed that the Trinitatis Sundays would soon change to the Advent Sundays. In the old country this was the time for the housewife to think of holiday preparations such as baking *Lebkuchen, Springerlei,* and other Christmas goodies that improved with age.

❖

In 1874 there were no near, neighborly housewives who were also making Christmas plans and with whom one could exchange ideas; no shops to visit; no evergreens to conjure up pictures of holiday splendor; and nothing in the soddie with which to make fitting gifts.

Fortunately the children were still so engrossed with their "bon voyage" presents that in spite of the snow, Christmas was not holding the usual importance in their childish thoughts and play. But when they helped their mother set up the Christmas twigs, the two little sisters were reminded of similar preparations for the holidays in Russia and asked, "Will Christmas come on the prairie so far from Russia and Grandfather and Grandmother?"

It was more because of habit than of faith in what she did, that Codray had cut willows and arranged them in a crock on the kitchen window near the adobe stove. In fruitful south Russia, she, like her mother before her, had always cut peach or cherry twigs and by soaking them in warm water had forced them to blossom for the coming of the Christ Child. On the Dakota prairie there were no fruit trees for Christmas bloom—only here and there a few willows by a shallow lake or slow-flowing creek. In this new country what outward signs for Christmas could they substitute for the dear, familiar symbols of old country Christmas celebration?

It was clear to these pioneer parents that a prairie Christmas could not be an elaborate celebration like in Russia, but they were sure it could be a Christmas celebration nevertheless. They assured the children that the Christ Child would come to good children no matter where they lived. Content that Christmas would come because Father and Mother had said so, the two sisters began to wonder what *Kristkindle* and *Pelznickel* would bring them if they were diligent and learned the lessons and did the tasks that Father and Mother set for them. From their superior knowledge of four and six Christmases they tried to impress upon their 2-year-old brother all the joys of the holiday season.

The children were delighted with the blooming of the Christmas twigs. To them it was one more assurance that *Kristkindle* was coming. What if, instead of flowers, the willows had produced soft, fuzzy buds that looked very much like fur-wrapped Indian babies clinging to their mothers' backs? These little "papoose willows" became a pre-holiday source of much pleasure and excitement.

The problem of how to get a suitable Christmas tree was still unsolved, but Codray's attempt to foster the Christmas spirit in America with willows so heartened the family that Johannes thought he'd try his hand with the pliable osiers. But how could one make a beautiful Christmas tree out of a straight, uninspiring willow? "Graceful as a willow wand" might serve the poet, but how could it serve the pioneers whose children expected that tree of all trees, a Christmas tree with many heavily laden branches?

Johannes put on his Russian *Pelz* and tall fur cap and went down to the lakeshore. There he selected a straight, stout willow about the thickness of his thumb and hoped for inspiration. He took it to his workbench, bored holes into it about where branches could be and whittled down willow tips to fit the holes. In spite of the make-believe branches, it was only a bare, stiff, ungainly tree skeleton, but somehow there was an innate, sturdy courage about it, and who could say that the Christmas spirit was not in its heart?

Codray was completely surprised when her husband showed her what he had done out at the workbench. "Can we make a willow blossom like a Christmas tree?" he paraphrased apologetically.

For a moment his wife was really dismayed by the unchristmas-like tree. But its meek, comical, scarecrow appearance touched her heart, and its utter forlornness aroused her maternal instinct. She wanted something with which to cover its nakedness. "Of course we can make it blossom like a Christmas tree," she said, talking to keep up her courage until she could think of something to do. "We haven't the abundance of Russia, but hasn't God blessed all our efforts? Didn't we take what the prairie had to offer and make a warm sod house? Buffalo chips and prairie grass have furnished fuel, wild fowls and fish have been our food. Surely a Christmas tree is not impossible when the spirit of Christmas is abroad. Just come with me and we will make it blossom." And she led the way back to the house.

In the soddie the homesteaders collected every scrap of plain paper they could find. Even the margins of the few treasured copies of the pioneer newspaper, the *Dakota Freie Presse,* were sacrificed. Codray went to the homemade cupboard and unwrapped her winter's supply of Frank's chicory. Many settlers used chicory as a coffee substitute. She soaked the brilliant red wrapper in water to extract the color. Into the red dye-bath she dipped the scraps of paper. When they were dry she cut the colored pieces into fringe and carefully, lovingly twisted them around each stiff, make-believe willow branch. All left-over scraps were fashioned into rosettes for ornamenting the tips of the branches. Such a Christmas tree as was "never seen on land or sea" began to blossom in the prairie soddie. The tree was its own inspiration for presents. A willow with a twisted root was fashioned into a hobby horse for little brother. But it looked so lonesome that Johannes made hobby horses for each of the girls also. Willow whistles and tops suggested themselves.

Since Christmas and dolls are almost synonymous in the minds of little girls, dolls would have to be produced somehow. Dolls? Codray thought of cookie dolls. They would be novelties. But a novelty is usually short-lived, and among children with good teeth and healthy appetites, edible novelties would not last long. Then, though their tummies might feel full, their hearts would be empty after Christmas day. Codray would have to devise more substantial dolls. Would the Christmas tree give the inspiration?

After the children were asleep in their trundle bed, the parents brought the tree into the house and worked on their Christmas preparations. Their little willow emblem of Christmas stood up courageously and tried its best to fill the exalted position for which it was destined. Surely they could not fail the tree or the children who placed such confidence in them. They had used willows for fuel, for fishpoles, for rabbit snares, for brooms, for baskets, and now for a Christmas tree. Why not willow dolls in keeping with their prairie Christmas motif?

The young mother took a bunch of slender willow-tips and tied them together for the body of the doll. Her skillful fingers fashioned a cloth-covered head and her husband whittled the arms. When dressed, "Willowminna Americana" was very intriguing indeed. To keep "Willowminna" from being lonesome, Codray started to make a whole family of willow dolls and a Russian "Ami" to help care for them. She clapped her hands with delight when her husband evened the tips of the willows and stood the dolls in a row on the drop-leaf table. The little girls surely would enjoy dolls that could stand.

As the homesteaders surveyed the row of dolls, they noticed that the oil in the glass lamp was getting low. They knew there would be no chance to replenish the one gallon of kerosene oil before spring. But this was Christmas. It would take another evening or two to complete the doll family and the willow trundle bed that Johannes had suggested. So the happy parents decided to work on and forget for the time being all the difficulties of pioneering. After the holidays they could conserve kerosene and use only the wild goose lamp, the prairie substitute for the whale oil lamp of New England's pioneer days.

The wild goose lamp—a wick soaked in melted goose fat—was a greasy, sputtering, sooty affair at its best, but it gave sufficient light during the short evenings that the homesteaders allowed themselves for basket weaving, harness oiling, plowshare polishing, wool carding, and such other pioneer occupations that depended as much on touch as on sight.

On the last evening of their Christmas preparations, Codray sat close to the brightly polished glass lamp and sewed up the little doll feather ticks and pillow cases that she and her husband had filled with wild goose feathers. Then from the tin foil that had been carefully saved from Johannes' tobacco, they shaped two little cups and two little saucers for a tea set, and covered a few nuts with the remaining tin foil.

Fervently Johannes wished there were more nuts and candies. But in October, when on one of the infrequent trips to Yankton, the storekeeper had suggested to the immigrant that it might be well to make some purchases for Christmas, Johannes could not take it seriously. Who can get into the Christmas spirit when days are warm and the sun is shining brightly? But because the storekeeper suggested it, Johannes made a few desultory purchases. He felt awkward about it, for he and his wife had always gone to Odessa together for Christmas shopping. Now alone he did not know just what to buy. Of course, candy and nuts were essential to Christmas cheer so he bought some, thinking to get more when his wife would be with him on the next trip. But the early snows had prevented any more trips to Yankton. So, the few tin foil nuts and the red rosettes made from the paper scraps would have to make as grand a showing as possible on the Christmas tree. There would be no candles. Wild goose candles were out of the question, and there was no tallow.

Although it was late when finally the few nuts had been fastened on the tree, the rosettes adjusted, and the tree returned to the workbench, yet Codray took time to set the sponge for the day-before-Christmas baking and Johannes laid the fire in the adobe stove, before they retired.

The next morning, after a breakfast of milk and "Gritz," Bevela and Katya, quivering with excitement, did the dishes to the tunes of "O du fröhliche" and "Von Himmel hoch" while their mother tended to the bread sponge. The singing was interrupted with many giggles and squeals of delight. For every time the dough gave a squeak as their mother worked it down, the girls had to join in and exclaim over how light and fine the Christmas goodies were going to be.

The white flour was very low in the barrel, but since it was Christmas and there was so little with which to celebrate, Codray trusted that the good Father in heaven would stretch the flour as He had the widow's supply of meal, and let them celebrate with extra goodies for the children and for the stranger who might come their way. What fun the two little sisters had putting raisin eyes on the dolls and animals and doves of peace that their mother made from dough. For the gifts that Codray desired to give and could not, she baked a dough replica and gave it in edible form.

In the middle of the afternoon, when the little sisters felt they could no longer be on their best behavior, there was a loud knocking on the door and *Pelznickel* with book and switch came in. He questioned the little girls about their conduct and examined them in their ABC's, asked what church hymns they could sing, whether they were learning to read and write and had started the shorter catechism. Having received favorable answers and impressions, *Pelznickel* gave each a few candies and nuts and a dove of peace carrying a little willow twig in its mouth. Since they were such good, studious children, he assured them, *"Kristkindle* will remember you on the morrow."

❖

Kristkindle came while the children slept.

On Christmas morning the little willow Christmas tree had a surprising array of gifts. Some looked so good that the children not only wanted to, but could eat them. Everyone had been remembered. Even the dog, Watch, had not been forgotten. When the children took him his cake of bran, it looked so appetizing that they shared it with him.

What a blessed Christmas morning! Cold and sparkling outside. Everything transformed with white shining brightness. The dry grass that had given the soddie a wild, shaggy look now made it look like a white loaf cake covered with coconut frosting. A few, large snowflakes lazily zig-zagged outside the window. The children thought they moved slowly to get a glimpse of the Christmas cheer in the soddie.

The children were delighted with their prairie Christmas tree. No one had ever seen such a tree. Nor such dolls! Dolls that could stand! Three hobby horses went a-prancing! Father taught the children how to spin the tops and blow the whistles. Mother gave each a tiny willow basket of nuts, candy, and cookies. Nowhere in all "Kristkindledom" were there three happier children than in the soddie on the Clear Lake homestead.

By eleven o'clock the Christmas wild goose was

roasting merrily in the adobe oven. Toys were laid aside. Since they could not go to the usual eleven o'clock Christmas morning church service, the family gathered around, and Father read the Christmas story, and together they sang the Christmas songs.

What a Christmas celebration! New world willow dolls, willow doll beds, willow whistles, willow tops, willow hobby horses, willow baskets, and a willow tree—a new world willow Christmas symphony, but the old world Christmas story and the old world Christmas songs.

And so it was "on Christmas day in the morning" out on the Dakota prairie in 1874.

The Gift of the Magi

O. HENRY

Whenever Christmas stories are shared, there are a few (so few they may be counted on the fingers of one hand) that, like cream, invariably rise to the top. Very few stories survive the generation they are written for; and fewer yet are alive for a third. Thus, to be around for a fourth presupposes an intangible something that remains undefinable. Of these lonely holdouts none is more beloved than this story.

William Sidney Porter, of Greens-

boro, North Carolina, became famous as O. Henry, chronicling those people forgotten by the literati. Society columnists might glorify the "400" elite who were worthy to be invited to a Vanderbilt fete, but, to O. Henry, the really important New Yorkers were the 4,000,000 who weren't invited. Representative of these 4,000,000 are the young and so very poor Mr. and Mrs. James Dillingham Young. No more unlikely candidates to Magi-hood could one imagine.

One dollar and eighty-seven cents. That was all. And 60 cents of it was in pennies. Pennies saved one and two at a time by bulldozing the grocer and the vegetable man and the butcher until one's cheeks burned with the silent imputation of parsimony that such close dealing implied. Three times Della counted it. One dollar and eighty-seven cents. And the next day would be Christmas.

There was clearly nothing to do but flop down on the shabby little couch and howl. So Della did it. Which instigates the moral reflection that life is made up of sobs, sniffles, and smiles, with sniffles predominating.

While the mistress of the home is gradually subsiding from the first stage to the second, take a look at the home. A furnished flat at $8 per week. It did not exactly beggar description, but it certainly had that word on the lookout for the mendicancy squad.

In the vestibule below was a letter-box into which no letter would go, and an electric button from which no mortal finger could coax a ring. Also appertaining thereunto was a card bearing the name "Mr. James Dillingham Young."

The "Dillingham" had been flung to the breeze during a former period of prosperity when its possessor was being paid $30 per week. Now, when the income was shrunk to $20, the letters of "Dillingham" looked blurred, as though they were thinking seriously of contracting to a modest and unassuming D. But whenever Mr. James Dillingham Young came home and reached his flat above he was called "Jim" and greatly hugged by Mrs. James Dillingham Young, already introduced to you as Della. Which is all very good.

Della finished her cry and attended to her cheeks with the powder rag. She stood by the window and looked out dully at a gray cat walking a gray fence in a gray backyard. Tomorrow would be Christmas Day, and she had only $1.87 with which to buy Jim a present. She had been saving every penny she could for months, with this result. Twenty dollars a week doesn't go far. Expenses had been greater than she had calculated. They always are. Only $1.87 to buy a present for Jim. Her Jim. Many a happy hour she had spent planning for something nice for him. Something fine and rare and sterling—something just a little bit near to being worthy of the honor of being owned by Jim.

There was a pier glass between the windows of the room. Perhaps you have seen a pier glass in an $8 flat. A very thin and very agile person may, by observing his reflection in a rapid sequence of longitudinal strips, obtain a fairly accurate conception of his looks. Della, being slender, had mastered the art.

Suddenly she whirled from the window and stood before the glass. Her eyes were shining brilliantly, but her face had lost its color within 20 seconds. Rapidly she pulled down her hair and let it fall to its full length.

Now, there were two possessions of the James Dillingham Youngs in which they both took a mighty pride. One was Jim's gold watch that had been his father's and his grandfather's. The other was Della's hair. Had the Queen of Sheba lived in the flat across the airshaft, Della would have let her hair hang out the window some day to dry just to depreciate Her Majesty's

❖

jewels and gifts. Had King Solomon been the janitor, with all his treasures piled up in the basement, Jim would have pulled out his watch every time he passed, just to see him pluck at his beard from envy.

So now Della's beautiful hair fell about her rippling and shining like a cascade of brown waters. It reached below her knees and made itself almost a garment for her. And then she did it up again nervously and quickly. Once she faltered for a minute and stood still while a tear or two splashed on the worn red carpet.

On went her old brown jacket; on went her old brown hat. With a whirl of skirts and with the brilliant sparkle still in her eyes, she fluttered out the door and down the stairs to the street.

Where she stopped the sign read: "Mme. Sofronie. Hair Goods of All Kinds." One flight up Della ran, and collected herself, panting. Madame, large, too white, chilly, hardly looked the "Sofronie."

"Will you buy my hair?" asked Della.

"I buy hair," said Madame. "Take yer hat off and let's have a sight at the looks of it."

Down rippled the brown cascade.

"Twenty dollars," said Madame, lifting the mass with a practiced hand.

"Give it to me quick," said Della.

Oh, and the next two hours tripped by on rosy wings. Forget the hashed metaphor. She was ransacking the stores for Jim's present.

She found it at last. It surely had been made for Jim and no one else. There was no other like it in any of the stores, and she had turned all of them inside out. It was a platinum fob chain simple and chaste in design, properly proclaiming its value by substance alone and not by meretricious ornamentation——as all good things should do. It was even worthy of The Watch. As soon as she saw it she knew that it must be Jim's. It was like him. Quietness and value——the description applied to both. Twenty-one dollars they took from her for it, and she hurried home with the 87 cents. With that chain on his watch Jim might be properly anxious about the time in any company. Grand as the watch was, he sometimes looked at it on the sly on account of the old leather strap that he used in place of a chain.

When Della reached home her intoxication gave way a little to prudence and reason. She got out her curling irons and lighted the gas and went to work repairing the ravages made by generosity added to love. Which is always a tremendous task, dear friends——a mammoth task.

Within 40 minutes her head was covered with

tiny, close-lying curls that made her look wonderfully like a truant schoolboy. She looked at her reflection in the mirror long, carefully, and critically.

"If Jim doesn't kill me," she said to herself, "before he takes a second look at me, he'll say I look like a Coney Island chorus girl. But what could I do—oh! what could I do with a dollar and eighty-seven cents?"

At 7 o'clock the coffee was made and the frying-pan was on the back of the stove hot and ready to cook the chops.

Jim was never late. Della doubled the fob chain in her hand and sat on the corner of the table near the door that he always entered. Then she heard his step on the stair away down on the first flight, and she turned white for just a moment. She had a habit of saying little silent prayers about the simplest everyday things, and now she whispered: "Please God, make him think I am still pretty."

The door opened and Jim stepped in and closed it. He looked thin and very serious. Poor fellow, he was only 22—and to be burdened with a family! He needed a new overcoat and he was without gloves.

Jim stopped inside the door, as immovable as a setter at the scent of quail. His eyes were fixed upon

Della, and there was an expression in them that she could not read, and it terrified her. It was not anger, nor surprise, nor disapproval, nor horror, nor any of the sentiments that she had been prepared for. He simply stared at her fixedly with that peculiar expression on his face.

Della wriggled off the table and went for him.

"Jim, darling," she cried, "don't look at me that way. I had my hair cut off and sold it because I couldn't have lived through Christmas without giving you a present. It'll grow out again—you won't mind, will you? I just had to do it. My hair grows awfully fast. Say 'Merry Christmas!' Jim, and let's be happy. You don't know what a nice—what a beautiful nice gift I've got for you."

"You've cut off your hair?" asked Jim, laboriously, as if he had not arrived at that patent fact yet even after the hardest mental labor.

"Cut it off and sold it," said Della. "Don't you like me just as well, anyhow? I'm me without my hair, ain't I?"

Jim looked about the room curiously.

"You say your hair is gone?" he said, with an air almost of idiocy.

"You needn't look for it," said Della. "It's sold, I

tell you—sold and gone, too. It's Christmas Eve, boy. Be good to me, for it went for you. Maybe the hairs of my head were numbered," she went on with a sudden serious sweetness, "but nobody could ever count my love for you. Shall I put the chops on, Jim?"

Out of his trance Jim seemed quickly to wake. He enfolded his Della. For 10 seconds let us regard with discreet scrutiny some inconsequential object in the other direction. Eight dollars a week or a million a year— what is the difference? A mathematician or a wit would give you the wrong answer. The magi brought valuable gifts, but that was not among them. This dark assertion will be illuminated later on.

Jim drew a package from his overcoat pocket and threw it upon the table.

"Don't make any mistake, Dell," he said, "about me. I don't think there's anything in the way of a haircut or a shave or a shampoo that could make me like my girl any less. But if you'll unwrap that package you may see why you had me going a while at first."

White fingers and nimble tore at the string and paper. And then an ecstatic scream of joy; and then, alas! a quick feminine change to hysterical tears and wails, necessitating the immediate employment of all the comforting powers of the lord of the flat.

For there lay The Combs—the set of combs, side and back, that Della had worshipped for long in a Broadway window. Beautiful combs, pure tortoise shell, with jeweled rims—just the shade to wear in the beautiful vanished hair. They were expensive combs, she knew, and her heart had simply craved and yearned over them without the least hope of possession. And now, they were hers, but the tresses that should have adorned the coveted adornments were gone.

But she hugged them to her bosom, and at length she was able to look up with dim eyes and a smile and say: "My hair grows so fast, Jim!"

And then Della leaped up like a little singed cat and cried, "Oh, oh!"

Jim had not yet seen his beautiful present. She held it out to him eagerly upon her open palm. The dull precious metal seemed to flash with a reflection of her bright and ardent spirit.

"Isn't it a dandy, Jim? I hunted all over town to find it. You'll have to look at the time a hundred times a day now. Give me your watch. I want to see how it looks on it."

Instead of obeying, Jim tumbled down on the

couch and put his hands under the back of his head and smiled.

"Dell," he said, "let's put our Christmas presents away and keep 'em a while. They're too nice to use just at present. I sold the watch to get the money to buy your combs. And now suppose you put the chops on."

The magi, as you know, were wise men—wonderfully wise men—who brought gifts to the Babe in the manger. They invented the art of giving Christmas presents. Being wise, their gifts were no doubt wise ones, possibly bearing the privilege of exchange in case of duplication. And here I have lamely related to you the uneventful chronicle of two foolish children in a flat who most unwisely sacrificed for each other the greatest treasures of their house. But in a last word to the wise of these days let it be said that of all who give gifts these two were the wisest. Everywhere they are wisest. They are the Magi.

Charlie's Blanket

❖

WENDY MILLER

It was a bitterly cold Canadian Christmas. Cold in more ways than one. Mary could see precious little to be thankful for, deserted as they had been by husband and father. Everywhere else but in their dreary little flat, Christmas took the cold away. Worst of all, the deadly acid of bitterness was gradually destroying the forsaken little family.

All but Becky, who was content with but a worn-out rag of a blanket——and Charlie.

Some months ago, as I opened my mail, I noticed a packet from Canada. Wendy Miller, a homemaker from Alberta, in her letter, said this about the story she enclosed: "This story really happened. Very few facts are changed at all. I did change our names, because I did not wish our family to be easily recognized. I know it's true, because I lived it, and Becky is my sister. I realize that the story is not very polished and maybe not even very good. I am not a writer. I do write a lot of stories and poetry, but only for my family; this is the first story I have ever shared with anyone else. The words just kind of went from heart to paper."

Mrs. Miller was modest. The text that follows needed very little editing. And the story . . . well, I guess the fact that it leapfrogged over all those other stories by well-known authors will tell you how it affected me.

Mary hurried to get her children fed and dressed. It was a cold December day, and they had a long way to walk. Mary cleaned houses five days a week; it was the only work she could find that would allow her to also take care of her three small girls at the same time. She would drop the older two off at the elementary school and take 3-year-old Becky with her. The girls came to her for lunch, and she would be back home again before they were home from school in the afternoon. It was a good arrangement, and it kept her off welfare. She wanted help from no one.

"Becky," she called, "hurry; we're all ready to go!"

Becky ran to the door, a ragged doll with all its hair loved off cradled in her arms. "I'm all ready, Mama, but we forgot to dress Charlie."

Mary glanced at the clock and back down at her daughter's smiling face. Quickly she dressed the doll, wrapped it in its blanket, and handed it back to Becky. Then the little family went out into the cold, dark early morning.

"Mama,"—Laura, 7, and the oldest, took Mary's hand—"I'm sorry I forgot Charlie. Are we awfully late?"

"No, Laura, we're not awfully late."

"I don't know why we have to dress that stupid doll of hers anyway," complained Cindy. Since she was 6 and in the first grade, she thought of herself as all grown up—and to her, Charlie was a big waste of time.

Two years ago Mary might have agreed with her. They had been well off then and wanted for nothing.

Mary's thoughts traveled back to other times and compared then to now as she had done a million times. One day everything was fine, and the next day her husband was gone. All he had left behind was a note to say goodbye. No, he had also left behind a wife, three small girls, and an empty bank account.

As soon as the shock had worn off, Mary tried to start a new life, but it was so hard. She had never had to work outside the home before. Now she was cleaning houses to keep the girls fed. Their clothes were handed down from her employers' children. Most of all she regretted having to make them walk so far every day, especially in the cold.

As for the radical change in lifestyle, the girls had just accepted it as part of life. Laura and Cindy helped as much as they could and tried not to complain. Becky found happiness in her doll. Charlie was her whole world. She never quit smiling as long as she had Charlie. He was always to be dressed for the weather and then wrapped in the precious blanket. It was just an old scrap of a blanket that somebody must have dropped in the parking lot; Becky found it there, Mary washed it, and now it was Charlie's. Was Charlie a waste of time? No, Mary decided; he was Becky's happiness, and that most certainly was not a waste of time.

As they neared the school, the girls hugged Mary

126

as they always did day after day, then ran in. Farther down the street, Mary turned in at the Littles'—Monday's house. The Littles had been getting ready for Christmas, it seemed, because there was a wreath on the door with a big red bow. Mary was prepared to see all the fancy trimmings inside. Becky wasn't.

"Ooh, Charlie," she whispered as if afraid that her voice might disturb the splendor, "look at what Mrs. Little got." The room was gaily decorated for Christmas, and in the corner stood a huge Christmas tree. The silver star shining on the top almost touched the ceiling. Glass ornaments, garlands, and tinsel were tastefully arranged on the branches, and underneath was a mountain of parcels wrapped with ribbons and bows.

Mary took Becky's coat and hung it up. The little girl just stood looking at the tree. "Becky, I have to get to work now. Promise you won't touch anything."

"I promise, Mama." And she crawled into a big easy chair, and there she stayed for the entire morning, pointing out the pretty ornaments to Charlie and guessing what might be in each of the packages.

Laura and Cindy came in at lunch, but they hardly looked at the tree. It hurt to look at it. They knew that there would be no tree for them—just like last year. Money was not to be spent on anything they could do without. They knew it—but it still hurt.

The day replayed itself on Tuesday at the Johnsons', on Wednesday at the Harrises', Thursday at the Krebbs', and Friday at the Fishers'. But on Saturday they were home.

After spending a week in the various houses all decked in glorious holiday fashion, Becky suddenly seemed to realize that she was missing out on something. "Why does everyone have a tree in the house, Mama? Why are there so many presents? Is it somebody's birthday? Why don't we have a tree?"

Mary had known the question would be asked. Laura and Cindy looked up from the floor where they were playing, waiting for her answer. Mary put away her mending and pulled Becky up onto her lap. "You're a very smart girl. It *is* somebody's birthday, and I'll tell you all about Him. His name is Jesus, and He was born Christmas Day." And Mary told the girls how it came to happen and why there is a Christmas.

Becky hugged Charlie close. "Ooh, the poor Baby. Was it very cold in the stable? I wouldn't want to sleep in a stable, would you? I wish I could go there and see it, though."

"We *can* see it," Mary said, and she put her daughter off her knee. "Girls, get your coats on. We're going for a walk."

Down the street was a church. Every Christmas

a large crèche was set up. There was a wooden stable full of straw and large ceramic figures. High above hung a star. The girls were awed by the simple but beautiful scene. It was just as Mary had said it was from the story in the Bible. Becky didn't want to leave even when the cold seeped through her clothing and made her shiver.

The next week was just as hard for them. Everywhere they went, it seemed that the world was taunting them with a Christmas that wasn't to be theirs. In the malls carols played, and parents loaded up with the latest toys and games. As Mary picked out economy packs of socks and underwear for the girls' gifts she tried not to look in the other carts. At Safeway she whipped through the express line with one lone pack of spaghetti for their Christmas dinner. She laughed at the long line-ups of people with their carts full of turkey and fixings. But the laugh was hollow, because she would have loved to be one of those standing in line. Outside, families shouted and laughed as they picked out what each considered the perfect tree and then strapped it to the roof of their car. Mary tried not to notice. It was Laura and Cindy that finally made her heart well over with bitterness.

Somehow, when you are an adult, you can take whatever is dished out. You take things in stride and make the best of a situation. But, oh how different it is when your child is hurting! Nothing hurts a mother more than the sorrow of her child. And that's how it was with Mary. The school was focused on Christmas, which was only to be expected in December. The teachers had the children making ornaments and stringing popcorn for their trees at home. They wrote letters to Santa. At recess, the children told of the gifts they were expecting. Laura and Cindy said nothing. They did as they were expected in class and tried to avoid the other children at recess. It was at home that they expressed their hurt and anger at the world for leaving them out of Christmas. So the bitterness grew in Mary from the heartache of her girls.

Every carol and decoration seemed to make her colder. Every Christmas card or call of "Merry Christmas" made her hate the season more. Laura and Cindy, taking the cue from their mother as children often do, developed the same attitude. Only little Becky was immune. She rocked Charlie in her arms and told him again and again about Baby Jesus, who was born in a stable. She begged the girls daily to take her to the church so she could see the story "for true." They would take her grudgingly and drag her back home long before she was finished looking.

Christmas morning came in a flurry of snow.

Laura and Cindy woke up cold. They ran into Mary's room and burrowed under the covers with her to warm up. Mary cuddled them close and kissed their foreheads.

"Merry Christmas," she said.

"Merry Christmas, Mama," they echoed.

"I'm afraid there aren't a lot of gifts for you girls, but you go wake up Becky, and you can open what there is," she said resignedly.

The girls jumped out of the bed and ran to get their sister while Mary got up and dressed. Too soon, they were back.

"Where *is* she, Mama? We can't find her!" The words hit Mary like a truck. The three raced through the house calling her name, checking every closet and corner. They checked the yard and the neighbor's yard. No Becky! They must have missed her when they checked the house, Mary thought. She never goes off alone. They searched the house again.

"Dear Lord, please help me find her," she prayed as she rechecked every spot a child could possibly be in. "I'm sorry for my selfishness. The gifts and the dinner that I prayed for are not important. Forget them and just give me back my Becky." She was frantic now.

Then she noticed Charlie. He was carefully positioned in a chair facing a window. Mary's heart raced with her thoughts. Charlie was *never* out of Becky's sight. And where was his blanket? Becky always insisted that his blanket be wrapped tightly around him at all times. Suddenly she *knew!*

"Stay here!" she admonished the girls as she flew out the door into the dark and snowy morning. Down the street she ran, until she could see the church. Then she slowed, and tears of release ran down her face as she caught sight of her daughter. The star from the crèche was shining down on the manger where Becky had climbed in and was busily covering the Baby Jesus with the ratty scrap of a blanket. As she neared, Mary could hear Becky talking:

"You must be cold. I knew the snow would be falling on You. This is Charlie's blanket, but we will give it to You. He has me to keep him warm." She looked up when she heard the footsteps. "Oh! Hi, Mama." Becky smiled her beautiful innocent smile. "I was afraid He might have thought we forgot about Him on His birthday."

Mary plucked her out of the straw and held her tight, the tears now raining unchecked. "I *did* forget, Honey. . . . Dear Lord, I'm sorry I forgot." Then she tenderly carried her daughter home, filled at last with Christmas joy.

With Christmas carols to cheer them on, they

132

hung the popcorn strings and ornaments on Mary's tallest houseplant. A star made of tin foil perched on the top. They put the presents underneath, and there was just enough to fit nicely under the little tree. And best of all, Mary made a birthday cake. With their hands joined around the table, they all sang "Happy Birthday, Dear Jesus, happy birthday to You. . . ."

As for Charlie, cradled tightly in Becky's arms— even without his blanket, he was warm.

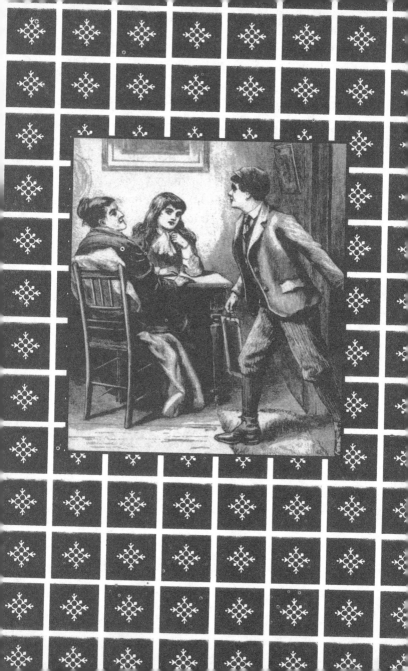

Star Across the Tracks

❖

BESS STREETER ALDRICH

"The wrong side of the tracks"——what an image that phrase conjures! Even in America, sad to say, those six words carry loaded freight: that anyone from the unfavored side is already prejudged, presorted, and predetermined. Perhaps "Can anything good come out of Nazareth" was an earlier equivalent of "living on the wrong side of the tracks."

Bess Streeter Aldrich (best known for her best-selling A Lantern in Her

Hand *and* A White Bird Flying), *along with Willa Cather, attempted to recreate in words just what it took for women to survive in Plains America. "Star Across the Tracks" is one of her most unforgettable short stories.*

❖ ❖ ❖

Mr. Harm Kurtz sat in the kitchen with his feet in the oven and discussed the world; that is to say, his own small world. His audience, shifting back and forth between the pantry and the kitchen sink, caused the orator's voice to rise and fall with its coming and going.

The audience was mamma. She was the bell upon which the clapper of his verbal output always struck. As she never stopped moving about at her housework during these nightly discourses, one might have said facetiously that she was his Roaming Forum.

Pa Kurtz was slight and wiry, all muscle and bounce. His wife had avoirdupois to spare and her leisurely walk was what is known in common parlance as a waddle. She wore her hair combed high, brushed

❖

tightly up at the back and sides, where it ended in a hard knot on top of her head. When movie stars and cafe society took it up, mamma said she had beat them to it by 35 years.

The Kurtzes lived in a little brown house on Mill Street, which meandered its unpaved way along a creek bed. The town, having been laid out by the founding fathers on this once-flowing but now long-dried creek, was called River City.

For three days of his working week pa's narrow world held sundry tasks: plowing gardens, cutting alfalfa, hauling lumber from the mill. For the other three days he was engaged permanently as a handyman by the families of Scott, Dillingham, and Porter, who lived on High View Drive, far away from Mill Street, geographically, economically, socially. And what mamma hadn't learned about the Scott, Dillingham, and Porter domestic establishments in the last few years wasn't worth knowing.

Early in his labors for the three families, pa had summed them up to mamma in one sweeping statement: "The Scotts . . . him I like and her I don't like. The Dillinghams . . . her I like and him I don't. The Porters . . . both I don't like."

The Porters' house was brick colonial. The

Scotts' was a rambling stone of the ranch type. The Dillinghams' had no classification, but was both brick and stone, to say nothing of stained shingles, lumber, tile, glass bricks, and stucco.

The Porters had four children of school age. Also they had long curving rows of evergreens in which the grackles settled with raucous glee as though to outvie the family's noise. The grackles—and for all pa knew, maybe the young folks also—drove Mrs. Porter wild, but pa rather like the birds. They sounded so country-like, and he had never grown away from the farm.

Mr. Porter was a lawyer and a councilman. Mrs. Porter was a member of the Garden Club and knew practically all there was to know about flora and fauna. She went in for formal beds of flowers, rectangles, and half-moons, containing tulips and daffodils in the spring and dahlias and asters later. She ruled pa with iron effi-ciency. With a wave of her hand she might say: "Mr. Kurtz, I think I'll have the beds farther apart this year."

And pa, telling mamma about it at night, would sneer: "Just like they was the springs-and-mattress kind you can shove around on casters."

Mrs. Scott went to the other extreme. She knew the least about vegetation of anyone who had ever come under

138

pa's scrutiny. Assuredly he was his own boss there. Each spring she tossed him several dozen packages of seeds as though she dared him to do his worst. Once he had found rutabaga and spinach among the packages of zinnias and nasturtiums. But pa couldn't be too hard on her, for she had a little crippled son who took most of her time. And he liked the fresh-colored packages every year and the feel of the warm moist earth when he put in the seeds. The head of the house was a doctor and if he happened to drive in while pa was there, he stopped and joked a bit.

The Dillinghams' yard was pa's favorite. The back of it was not only informal, it was woodsy. Mrs. Dillingham told pa she had been raised on a farm and that the end of the yard reminded her of the grove back of her old home. She had no children and often she came out to stand around talking to pa or brought her gloves and worked with him.

"Poor thing! Lonesome," mamma said at once when he was telling her.

Mrs. Dillingham had pa set out wild crab apple and ferns and plum trees, little crooked ones, so it would "look natural." Several times she had driven him out to the country and they had brought back shooting stars and swamp candle, Dutchman's-breeches and wood violets. Pa's hand with the little wild flowers was as tender as the hand of God.

When Mr. Dillingham came home from his big department store, he was loud and officious, sometimes critical of what had been done.

In winter, the work for the High View homes was just as hard and far less interesting. Storm windows, snow on long driveways, basements to be cleaned. It was always good to get home and sit with his tired, wet feet in the oven and tell the day's experiences to mamma. There was something very comforting about mamma, her consoling "Oh, think nothing of it," or her sympathetic clucking of "Tsk . . . tsk . . . them women, with their cars and their clubs!"

Tonight there was more than usual to tell, for there had been great goings on up in High View. Tomorrow night was Christmas Eve and in preparation for the annual prizes given by the federated civic clubs, his three families had gone in for elaborate outdoor decorations.

There was unspoken rivalry among the three houses, too. Pa could sense it. Mrs. Porter had asked him offhandedly, as though it were a matter of extreme unconcern, what the two other families were planning to do. And Mr. Dillingham had asked the same thing, but bluntly. You couldn't catch pa that way, though, he reminded mamma with great glee. "Slippery as a eel!" Had just answered that the others seemed to be hitchin' up a lot of wiring.

❖

But pa had known all along what each one was doing. And tomorrow night everybody would know. The Porters had long strings of blue lights, which they were carrying out into the evergreens, as though blue-birds, instead of black ones, were settling there to stay through Christmas.

The Dillinghams had gone in for reindeer. They had ordered them made from plyboard at the mill, and tonight the eight deer, with artificial snow all over them, were prancing up the porch steps, while a searchlight on the ground threw the group into relief.

The Scotts, whose house was not so high as the others, had a fat Santa on the roof with one foot in the chimney. In a near-by dormer window there was a phonograph which would play Jingle Bells, so that the song seemingly came from the old fellow himself. It had made the little crippled boy laugh and clap his hands when they wheeled him outside to see the fin-ished scene.

All this and much more pa was telling mamma while she ambled about, getting supper on the table.

Lillie came home. Lillie was the youngest of their three children and she worked for the Dillinghams, too, but in the department store. Lillie was a whiz with a needle, and a humble helper in the remodeling room. She made her own dresses at home and tried them on Maisie, the manikin. That was one of the store's moronic-looking models which had lost an arm and sundry other features, and Lillie had asked for it when she found they were going to discard it. Ernie, her brother, had brought it home in his car and repaired it. Now she hung her own skirts on Maisie to get their length. That was about all the good the manikin did her, for Lillie's circumference was fully three times that of the model.

The three of them sat down to eat, as Ernie would not arrive for a long time and mamma would warm things over for him. As usual, the table talk came largely from pa. He had to tell it all over to Lillie: the blue lights, the reindeer, the Santa-with-one-foot-in-the-chimney.

Lillie, who was a bit fed up with pasteboard reindeer and synthetic Santas at the store, thought she still would like to see them. So pa said tomorrow night after Carrie got here they would all drive to High View, that he himself would like to see them once from the paved street instead of with his head caught in an evergreen branch or getting a crick in his neck under a reindeer's belly.

They discussed the coming of the older daughter

and her husband, Bert, and the two little boys, who were driving here from their home in another county and planning to stay two whole nights. A big event was Christmas this year in the Mill Street Kurtz house.

After supper when Lillie started the dishes, pa went out to see to the team and mamma followed to pick out two of her fat hens for the Christmas dinner.

In the dusk of the unusually mild December evening, mamma stood looking about her as with the eye of a stranger. Then she said she wished things had been in better shape before Carrie and Bert got here, that not one thing had been done around the place to fix it up since the last time.

"That rickety old shed, pa," she said mildly. "I remember as well as I'm standin' here you tellin' Carrie you was goin' to have that good new lumber on by the next time she come."

It was as match to pine shavings. It made pa good and mad. With him working his head off, day and night! He blew up. In anyone under 12 it would have been called a tantrum. He rushed over to the tool house and got his hammer and started to yank off a rotten board.

"I'll get this done before Carrie comes," he shouted, "if it's the last thing I do."

A psychoanalyst, after much probing, might have

discovered what caused pa's sudden anger. But mamma, who knew less than nothing about psychoanalysis, having only good common sense, also knew what caused it.

Pa's own regrets over his big mistake made him irritable at times. He was one of those farmers who had turned their backs on old home places during the protracted drought. Mamma had wanted to stick it out another year, but he had said no, they would move to town where everybody earned good money. So they had sold the farm and bought this little place on Mill Street, the only section of town where one could keep a cow and chickens. The very next year crops were good again and now the man who had bought the old place for so little came to River City in a car as fine as the Dillinghams'. Yes, any casual criticism of the Mill Street place always touched him in a vital spot of his being. So he yanked and swore and jawed, more mad than ever that mamma had walked away and was not hearing him.

It was not hard to get the old boards off. Soon they lay on the ground in a scattered heap of rotting timbers. Bird and Bell, from their exposed position across the manger, snatched at the alfalfa hay, quivered their nostrils and looked disdainfully at proceedings. The cow chewed her cud in the loose-jawed way of cows and stared disinterestedly into space.

Looking at the animals of which he was so fond, pa admitted to himself he needn't have ripped the boards off until morning, but balmy weather was predicted all through Christmas. And mamma had made him pretty mad. Suddenly the fire of his anger went out, for he was remembering something Ernie had said and it tickled his fancy. The last time Carrie brought her little boys home, Ernie had told them it was bubble gum the cow was chewing and the kids had hung over the half door an hour or more waiting for the big bubble to blow out.

Tomorrow night the little kids would be here and the thought of it righted the world again.

Mamma came toward him with two hens under her arms as though she wanted him to make up with her. But he fussed around among the boards, not wanting to seem pleasant too suddenly.

His flashlight lay on the ground, highlighting the open shed, and the street light, too, shone in. An old hen flew squawking out of the hay and the pigeons swooped down from the roof.

Mamma stood looking at it for quite a while,

✤

then all at once she chucked the hens under a box and hurried into the house. When she came out, she held Maisie, the manikin, in front of her and Lillie was close behind with her arms full of sheets.

"What you think you're up to?" pa asked.

"You let me be," mamma said pointedly. "I know what I'm doin'."

She set up the manikin and with deft touches Lillie draped the sheets over its body and head and arranged it so it was leaning over the manger. Then mamma put pa's flashlight down in the manger itself and a faint light shone through the cracks of the old boards.

"There!" said mamma, stepping back. "Don't that look for all the world like the Bible story?"

"Seems like it's makin' light of it," pa said critically. "The Scotts and the Dillinghams didn't do nothin' like that. They just used Santy Clauses."

"I ain't doin' it for show, like them," mamma retorted. "I'm doin' it for Carrie's little boys. Somethin' they can see for themselves when they drive in. Somethin' they'll never forget, like's not, as long as they live."

Mamma and Lillie went out to the fence to survey their handiwork from that point. They were standing there when Ernie drove into the yard. Ernie worked for the River City Body and Fender Wreck Company, and one viewing the car and hearing its noisy approach would have questioned whether he ever patronized his own company.

They were anxious to know what Ernie thought. There were the horses nuzzling the alfalfa, the cow chewing away placidly, and the pigeons on the ridge-pole. And there was the white-robed figure bending over the faint glow in the manger.

Ernie stood without words. Then he said "For gosh sakes! What in time?" The words were crude, but the tone was reverent.

"Mamma did it for the kids," Lillie said. "She wants you to fix a star up over the stable. Mrs. Dilling-ham gave an old one to pa."

Ernie had been a fixer ever since he was a little boy. Not for his looks had the River City Body and Fender Wreck Company hired Ernie Kurtz. So after his warmed-over supper he got his tools and a coil of wire and fixed the yellow bauble high over the stable, the wire and the slim rod almost invisible, so that it seemed a star hung there by itself.

❖

❖

All the next day pa worked up on High View Drive and all day mamma cleaned the house, made doughnuts and cookies with green sugar on them, and dressed the fat hens, stuffing them to the bursting point with onion dressing.

Almost before they knew it, Christmas Eve had arrived, and Carrie and Bert and the two little boys were driving into the yard with everyone hurrying out to greet them.

"Why, mamma," Carrie said. "That old shed . . . it just gave me a turn when we drove in."

But mamma was a bit disappointed over the little boys. The older one comprehended what it meant and was duly awe-struck, but the younger one ran over to the manger and said: "When's she goin' to blow out her bubble gum?"

After they had taken in the wrapped presents and the mince pies Carrie had baked, pa told them how they were all going to drive up to High View and see the expensive decorations, stressing his own part in their preparation so much that mamma said, "Don't brag. A few others had somethin' to do with it, you know." And Ernie sent them all into laughter when he called it High Brow Drive.

❖

Then he went after his girl, Annie Hansen, and when they came back, surprisingly her brother was with them, which sent Lillie into a state of fluttering excitement.

So they all started out in two cars. Ernie and his girl and Lillie in Ernie's one seat, with the brother in the back, his long legs dangling out. Carrie and Bert took their little boys and mamma and pa. Not knowing the streets leading to the winding High View section, Bert stayed close behind Ernie's car, which chugged its way ahead of them like a noisy tugboat.

Everyone was hilariously happy. As for pa, his anger about mamma's chidings was long forgotten. All three of his children were home and the two little kids. The Dillinghams didn't have any children at all for Christmas fun. *We never lost a child,* he was thinking, *and the Porters lost that little girl. Our grandkids tough as tripe, and the Scotts got that crippled boy.* It gave him a light-hearted feeling of freedom from disaster. Now this nice sightseeing trip in Bert's good car. Home to coffee and doughnuts, with the kids hanging up their stockings. Tomorrow the presents and a big dinner. For fleeting moments Pa Kurtz had a warm little-boy feeling of his own toward Christmas.

Mamma, too, said she hadn't had such a good time since Tige was a pup. And when one of the little boys said he wanted to see Tige when they got back, everyone laughed immoderately.

They passed decorated houses and countless trees brightly lighted in windows. Then around the curving streets of the High View district, following Ernie's noisy lead so closely that Carrie said they were just like Mary's little lamb. Across the street from the Porters' colonial house, Ernie stopped, and they stopped too.

The evergreens with their sparkling blue lights seemed a part of an enchanted forest. Carrie said she never saw anything so pretty in her life and waxed so enthusiastic that pa reminded her again of his big part in it.

When Ernie yelled back to ask if they'd seen enough, pa waved him on. And around the curve they went to the Dillinghams'.

There were other cars in front of the houses. Pa said like as not the judges themselves were right now deciding the prizes, and by the tone of his voice one would have thought the fate of the nation hung on the decision.

At the Dillinghams', the little boys waxed more excited over the reindeer, lighted by the searchlight which threw them into snow-white relief. Yes, pa said, it was worth all the work they'd put on them.

Then to Doctor Scott's, and here the little boys practically turned inside out. For Santa himself was up on the roof as plain as day; and more, he was singing "Jingle bells, jingle bells." When he stopped, they clapped their hands and yelled up at him: "Hi, Santy! Sing more." And the adults all clapped too.

Then Ernie signaled and the little procession swung down out of High View and circled into the part of town where the blocks were prosaically rectangular and everything became smaller; yards, houses, Christmas trees.

"Look!" mamma said happily. "Ain't it nice? There ain't no patent on it. Everyone can make merry. Every little house can have its own fun and tree, just the same as the big ones."

Over the railroad tracks they went and into Mill Street, where Ernie adroitly picked his way around the mushy spots in the unpaved road, with Bert following his zigzag lead. And the trip was over.

There were Bird and Bell and the cow. There were the pigeons huddled together on the stable roof. There were the white Mary and the light in the manger, and the star. The laughter died down. Everyone got out quietly. Carrie ran her arm through her mother's. "I like yours, too, mamma," she said.

Inside, they grew merry again. Over the doughnuts and sandwiches there was a lot of talk. They argued noisily about the prize places for the decorated houses, betting one another which ones would win. Carrie and Lillie both thought the lights in the trees were by far the most artistic. Ma and Ernie's girl were for the reindeer at Dillinghams'. But Lillie's potential beau and Ernie and Bert and the little boys were all for the Scotts' Santa Claus. Pa, as one who had been the creator of them all, stayed benignly neutral.

After a while Ernie took his girl home. Her brother stood around on the porch awhile with Lillie and then left. The little boys hung up their stockings, with the grown folks teasing them, saying Santy could never find his way from the Scotts' down those winding streets.

Mamma and pa kept their own bedroom. Lillie took Carrie in with her. Bert made the little boys a bed on the old couch, with three chairs in front to keep them from falling out. She had no sheets left for them, but plenty of clean patchwork quilts.

In the morning there were the sketchy breakfast and the presents, including a dishpan for mamma, who had never had a new one since her wedding day; the bit and braces pa had wished for so long; a flowered comb-

and-brush set for Lillie; and fully one-third of the things for which the little boys had wished.

The children could play with their new toys and the men pitch horseshoes, but mamma and the girls had to hop right into the big dinner, for everyone would be starved. Ernie's girl and her brother were invited, too, and when they came, said they could smell that good dressing clear out in the yard. The hens practically popped open in the pans and mamma's mashed potatoes and gravy melted in the mouth. Oh, never did anyone have a nicer Christmas than the Kurtzes down on Mill Street.

It was when they were finishing Carrie's thick mince pies that the radio news came on, and the announcement of the prizes. So they pulled back their chairs to listen, with the girls cautioning the menfolks, "Now stick to what your bet was last night and don't anybody cheat by changing."

The announcer introduced the committee head, who gave a too wordy talk about civic pride. Then the prizes:

"The third prize of ten dollars to Doctor Amos R. Scott, 1821 High View Drive." That was Santa-in-the-chimney. And while Ernie and his group groaned their disappointment that it was only third, the others laughed at them for their poor bet.

❖

"The second—25 dollars—Mr. Ramsey E. Porter, 1484 High View Drive." The blue lights! With Carrie and Lillie wanting to know what the judges were thinking of, for Pete's sake, to give it only second, and mamma and Ernie's girl calling out jubilantly that it left only their own choice, the reindeer.

Then a strange thing happened.

"Listen, everybody."

"Sh! What's he saying?"

"The first prize . . . for its simplicity . . . for using materials at hand without expense . . . for its sacred note and the fact that it is the personification of the real Christmas story of which we sometimes lose sight . . . the first prize of 50 dollars is unanimously awarded to Mr. Harm Kurtz at 623 Mill Street."

A bomb would have torn fissures in the yard and made an unmendable shambles of the house, but it could not have been more devastating.

For a long moment they sat stunned, mouths open, but without speech coming forth, and only the little boys saying: "He said you, grandpa; he said you."

Then the hypnotic spell broke and Ernie let out a yell: "Fifty bucks, pa! Fifty bucks!"

And mamma, still dazed, kept repeating like some mournful raven, "But I just did it for the little boys."

❖

Several got up and dashed over to the window to see again this first-prize paragon. But all they could see was bird and Bell and the cow out in their little yard, an old dilapidated shed, and high up over it a piece of yellow glass.

In the midst of the excitement pa practically turned pale. For it had come to him suddenly there was more to this than met the eye. What would the Scotts and the Porters and the Dillinghams say? Especially Mr. Dillingham, whose expensive reindeer had won no prize at all. He was embarrassed and worried. The joy had gone out of winning the prize. The joy had gone out of the day.

The girls had scarcely finished the dishes before the Mill Street neighbors started coming to have a share in the big news. The Danish Hansens came and the Russian family from the next block, all three of the Czech families down the street, and the Negro children who lived near the mill. They were all alike to mamma. "Just folks." She gave everyone a doughnut. In fact, they ate so many, that late in the afternoon she whipped up another batch. Also, out of honor to the great occasion, she combed her hair again in that high skinned-up way and put on a second clean apron. Two clean aprons in one day constituted the height of something or other.

"Somebody might come by," she said by way of apology.

"They'll get stuck in the mud if they do," said Ernie. "I'm the only one that knows them holes like a map."

Mamma was right. Somebody came by. All River City came by.

Soon after dusk, with the star lighted and Bird and Bell back in the shed, the cars began to drive past in unending parade. Traffic was as thick as it had ever been up on Main and Washington. You could hear talk and laughter and maybe strong words about the mud holes. Then in front of the yard, both the talk and the laughter would die down, and there would be only low-spoken words or silence. Bird and Bell pulling at the hay. The cow gazing moodily into space. The pigeons on the ridgepole in a long feathery group. White Mary bending over a faint glow in the manger. And overhead the star.

In silence the cars would drive away and more come to take their places.

Three of them did not drive away. They swung in closer to the fence and all the people got out and came into the yard. Of all things!

"Mamma, there come the Scotts and the Porters and the Dillinghams." Pa was too excited for words and hardly knew what he was doing.

But mamma was cool and went out to meet them. "Sh! They're just folks, too."

The Scotts were lifting the wheeled chair out of the car, which had been custom built for it. Doctor Scott wheeled the little boy up closer so he could see the animals. Carrie's little boys ran to him and with the tactlessness of children showed him how they could turn cartwheels all around his chair.

"Why, Mr. Kurtz," Mrs. Porter was saying, "you're the sly one. Helping us all the time and then copping out the prize yourself."

Pa let it go. They would just have to believe it was all his doings, but for a fleeting moment he saw himself yanking madly at the shed boards.

Mrs. Her-I-don't-like Scott said, "It's the sweetest thing I ever saw. It made me feel like crying when I saw it."

Mrs. Dillingham said it made their decorations all look cheap and shoddy by the side of the manger scene. Even Mr. Dillingham, who had won no prize, said, "Kurtz, you certainly deserve it."

Pa knew he couldn't take any more praise. At least, not with mamma standing right there. So he said,

"I guess it was mamma's idea. She's always gettin' ideas."

Right then mamma had another one. "Will you all please to step inside and have a cup of coffee and a doughnut?"

The women demurred, but all the men said they certainly would.

So they crowded into the kitchen, mink coats and all, and stood about with coffee and doughnuts. And Lillie got up her courage and said to Mr. Dillingham, "I don't suppose you know me, but I work for you."

"Oh, yes, sure; sure I do," he said heartily, but Lillie knew he was only being polite.

"And this is a friend of mine," she added with coy bravado, "Mr. Hansen."

Mr. Dillingham said, "How do you do, Mr. Hansen. Don't tell me you work for me, too."

"Yes, sir, I do," said Lillie's new beau. "Packing."

And High View and Mill Street both laughed over it.

Mrs. Scott said, "Did you ever taste anything so good as these doughnuts? You couldn't find time to make me a batch once a week, could you?" So that Mrs. Dillingham and Mrs. Porter both said quickly, "Not unless she makes me one, too."

And mamma, pleased as Punch, but playing hard to catch, said maybe she could.

Mr. Porter was saying to Ernie, "You folks ought to have some gravel down here on Mill Street."

And Ernie, who wasn't afraid of anyone, not even a councilman, said with infinite sarcasm, "You're telling me?"

The big cars all drove away. Three or four others straggled by. Then no more. And pa turned off the light of the star.

The house was still again except for the adenoidal breathing of one of the little boys. Even Ernie, coming in late, stopped tromping about upstairs. Everyone had to get up early to see Bert and Carrie off and get back to work. It made pa worry over his inability to get to sleep. This had been the most exciting day in years.

Mamma was lying quietly, her heavy body sagging down her side of the bed. It took all pa's self-control to pretend sleep. Twice he heard the old kitchen clock strike another hour. He would try it.

"Mamma," he called softly.

"What?" she said instantly.

"Can't get to sleep."

"Wha's the matter?"

"Keep thinkin' of everything. All that money comin' to us. Company. Attention from so many folks. Children all home. Folks I work for all here and not a bit mad. You'd think I'd feel good. But I don't. Somethin' hangs over me. Like they'd been somebody real out there in the shed all this time; like we'd been leavin' 'em stay out when we ought to had 'em come on in. Fool notion—but keeps botherin' me."

And then mamma gave her answer. Comforting, too, just as he knew it would be. "I got the same feelin'. I guess people's been like that ever since it happened. Their conscience always hurtin' 'em a little because there wa'n't *no room for Him in the inn.*"

The Candle in the Forest

❖

TEMPLE BAILEY

In each collection there has been a mandated item: "You must include this story." This story represents the No. 1 mandate of the third collection. It is an old story that had almost been forgotten. But here and there were those who, having once heard it, were incapable of forgetting it, for it had warmed their hearts through all the years.

I cry every time I read it.

It reminds us that wealth may be

measured in many ways; so can poverty. Often, either is merely
a matter of perspective.

What a joy it is to bring back from the edge of extinction such a wondrous story! It was written by Temple Bailey, author of some of the most moving Christmas stories ever penned. This one, once read, is virtually impossible to forget.

The small girl's mother was saying, "The onions will be silver, and the carrots will be gold——"

"And the potatoes will be ivory," said the small girl, and they laughed together. The small girl's mother had a big white bowl in her lap, and she was cutting up vegetables. The onions were the hardest, because she cried over them.

"But our tears will be pearls," said the small girl's mother, and they laughed at that and dried their eyes, and found the carrots much easier, and the potatoes the easiest of all.

Then the next-door-neighbor came in and said, "What are you doing?"

"We are making a vegetable pie for our Christmas dinner," said the small girl's mother.

"And the onions are silver, and the carrots are gold, and the potatoes are ivory," said the small girl.

"I am sure I don't know what you are talking about," said the next-door-neighbor. "We are going to have turkey for dinner, and cranberries and celery."

The small girl laughed and clapped her hands. "But we are going to have a Christmas pie—and the onions will be silver and the carrots gold—"

"You said that once," said the next-door-neighbor, "and I should think you'd know they weren't anything of the kind."

"But they are," said the small girl, all shining eyes and rosy cheeks.

"Run along, darling," said the small girl's mother, "and find poor Pussy-purr-up. He's out in the cold. And you can put on your red sweater and red cap."

So the small girl hopped away like a happy robin, and the next-door-neighbor said, "She's old enough to know that onions aren't silver."

"But they are," said the small girl's mother. "And carrots are gold and the potatoes are—"

The next-door-neighbor's face was flaming. "If you say that again, I'll scream. It sounds silly to me."

"But it isn't in the least silly," said the small girl's mother, and her eyes were blue as sapphires, and as clear as the sea; "it is sensible. When people are poor, they have to make the most of little things. And we'll have only inexpensive things in our pie, but the onions will be silver—"

The lips of the next-door-neighbor were folded in a thin line. "If you had acted like a sensible creature, I shouldn't have asked you for the rent."

The small girl's mother was silent for a moment; then she said, "I am sorry—it ought to be sensible to make the best of things."

"Well," said the next-door-neighbor, sitting down in a chair with a very stiff back, "a pie is a pie. And I wouldn't teach a child to call it anything else."

"I haven't taught her to call it anything else. I was only trying to make her feel that it was something fine and splendid for Christmas Day, so I said that the onions were silver—"

"Don't say that again," snapped the next-door-neighbor, "and I want the rent as soon as possible."

With that, she flung up her head and marched out the front door, and it slammed behind her and made wild echoes in the little home.

And the small girl's mother stood there alone in the middle of the floor, and her eyes were like the sea in a storm.

But presently the door opened, and the small girl, looking like a red-breast robin, hopped in, and af-

166

ter her came a great black cat with his tail in the air, and he said, "Purr-up," which gave him his name.

And the small girl said, out of the things she had been thinking, "Mother, why don't we have turkey?"

The clear look came back into the eyes of the small girl's mother, and she said, "Because we are content."

And the small girl said, "What is content?"

And her mother said, "It is making the best of what God gives us. And our best for Christmas Day, my darling, is our Christmas pie."

So she kissed the small girl, and they finished peeling the vegetables, and then they put them to simmer on the back of the stove.

After that, the small girl had her supper of bread and milk, and Pussy-purr-up had milk in a saucer on the hearth, and the small girl climbed up in her mother's lap and said, "Tell me a story."

But the small girl's mother said, "Won't it be nicer to talk about Christmas presents?"

And the small girl sat up and said, "Let's."

And the mother said, "Let's tell each other what we'd rather have in the whole wide world."

"Oh, let's," said the small girl. "And I'll tell you

167
❧

first that I want a doll—and I want it to have a pink dress—and I want it to have eyes that open and shut—and I want it to have shoes and stockings—and I want it to have curly hair—" She had to stop, because she didn't have any breath left in her body, and when she got her breath back, she said, "Now, what do you want, Mother, more than anything else in the whole wide world?"

"Well," said the mother, "I want a chocolate mouse."

"Oh," said the small girl scornfully, "I shouldn't think you'd want that."

"Why not?"

"Because a chocolate mouse isn't anything."

"Oh, yes, it is," said the small girl's mother. "A chocolate mouse is Dickory-Dock, and Pussy-Cat-Pussy-Cat-where-have-you-been-was-frightened-under-a-chair, and the mice in Three-Blind-Mice ran after the farmer's wife, and the mouse in A-Frog-Would-a-Wooing-Go went down the throat of the crow—"

And the small girl said, "Could a chocolate mouse do all that?"

"Well," said the small girl's mother, "we could put him on the clock, and under a chair, and cut his tail with a carving knife, and at the very last we could eat him like a crow—"

The small girl said, shivering deliciously, "And he wouldn't be a real mouse?"

"No, just a chocolate one, with cream inside."

"Do you think I'll get one for Christmas?"

"I'm not sure," said the mother.

"Would he be nicer than a doll?"

The small girl's mother hesitated, then told her the truth. "My darling, Mother saved up money for a doll, but the next-door-neighbor wants the rent."

"Hasn't Daddy any more money?"

"Poor Daddy has been sick so long."

"But he's well now."

"I know. But he has to pay for the doctors, and money for medicine, and money for your red sweater, and money for milk for Pussy-purr-up, and money for our pie."

"The boy-next-door says we're poor, Mother."

"We are rich, my darling. We have love, each other, and Pussy-purr-up—"

"His mother won't let him have a cat," said the small girl, with her mind still on the boy-next-door. "But he's going to have a radio."

"Would you rather have a radio than Pussy-purr-up?"

The small girl gave a crow of derision. "I'd rather

have Pussy-purr-up than anything else in the whole wide world."

At that, the great cat, who had been sitting on the hearth with his paws tucked under him and his eyes like moons, stretched out his satin-shining length and jumped up on the arm of the chair beside the small girl and her mother, and began to sing a song that was like a mill-wheel away off. He purred to them so loud and so long that at last the small girl grew drowsy.

"Tell me some more about the chocolate mouse," she said, and nodded, and slept.

The small girl's mother carried her into another room, put her to bed, and came back to the kitchen, and it was full of shadows.

But she did not let herself sit among them. She wrapped herself in a great cape and went out into the cold dusk. There was a sweep of wind, heavy clouds overhead, and a band of dull orange showing back of the trees, where the sun had burned down.

She went straight from her little house to the big house of the next-door-neighbor and rang the bell at the back entrance. A maid let her into the kitchen, and

170

there was the next-door-neighbor, and the two women who worked for her, and a daughter-in-law who had come to spend Christmas. The great range was glowing, and things were simmering, and things were stewing, and things were steaming, and things were baking, and things were boiling, and things were broiling, and there were the fragrances of a thousand delicious dishes in the air.

And the next-door-neighbor said: "We are trying to get as much done as possible tonight. We have plans for 12 people for Christmas dinner tomorrow."

And the daughter-in-law, who was all dressed up and had an apron tied about her, said in a sharp voice, "I can't see why you don't let your maids work for you."

And the next-door-neighbor said: "I have always worked. There is no excuse for laziness."

And the daughter-in-law said, "I'm not lazy, if that's what you mean. And we'll never have any dinner if I have to cook it." And away she went out of the kitchen with tears of rage in her eyes.

And the next-door-neighbor said, "If she hadn't gone when she did, I should have told her to go," and there was rage in her eyes but no tears.

She took her hands out of the pan of bread

crumbs and sage, which was being mixed for the stuffing, and said to the small girl's mother, "Did you come to pay the rent?"

The small girl's mother handed her the money, and the next-door-neighbor went upstairs to write a receipt. Nobody asked the small girl's mother to sit down, so she stood in the middle of the floor and sniffed the entrancing fragrances, and looked at the mountain of food that would have served her small family for a month.

While she waited, the boy-next-door came in and said, "Are you the small girl's mother?"

"Yes."

"Are you going to have a tree?"

"Yes."

"Do you want to see mine?"

"It would be wonderful."

So he led her down a long passage to a great room, and there was a tree that touched the ceiling, and on the very top branches and on all the other branches were myriads of little lights that shone like stars, and there were gold bells and silver ones, and red and blue and green balls, and under the tree and on it were toys for boys and toys for girls, and one of the toys was a doll in a pink dress! At that, the heart of the small girl's mother tightened, and she was glad she wasn't a thief, or she would have snatched at the pink doll when the boy wasn't looking, and hidden it under her cape, and run away with it.

The next-door-neighbor-boy was saying, "It's the finest tree anybody has around here. But Dad and Mother don't know that I've seen it."

"Oh, don't they?" said the small girl's mother.

"No," said the boy-next-door, with a wide grin, "and it's fun to fool 'em."

"Is it?" said the small girl's mother. "Now, do you know, I should think the very nicest thing in the whole world would be not to have seen the tree."

"Because," said the small girl's mother, "the nicest thing in the world would be to have somebody tie a handkerchief around your eyes, so tight, and then to have somebody take your hand and lead you in and out, and in and out, and in and out, until you didn't know where you were, and then to have them untie the hand-kerchief—and there would be the tree, all shining and splendid!" She stopped, but her singing voice seemed to echo and re-echo in the great room.

The boy's staring eyes had a new look in them. "Did anybody ever tie a handkerchief over your eyes?"

"Oh, yes—"

173

❖

"And lead you in and out, and in and out?"

"Yes."

"Well, nobody does things like that in our house. They think it's silly."

The small girl's mother laughed, and her laugh tinkled like a bell. "Do you think it's silly?"

He was eager. "No, I don't."

She held out her hand to him. "Will you come and see our tree?"

"Tonight?"

"No, tomorrow morning—early."

"Before breakfast?"

She nodded.

"I'd like it!"

So that was a bargain, and with a quick squeeze of their hands on it. And the small girl's mother went back to the kitchen, and the next-door-neighbor came down with the receipt, and the small girl's mother went out the back door and found that the orange band that had burned on the horizon was gone, and that there was just the wind and the singing of the trees.

Two men passed her on the brick walk that led to

the house, and one of the men was saying, "If you'd only be fair to me, Father."

And the other man said, "All you want of me is money."

"You taught me that, Father."

"Blame it on me——"

"You are to blame. You and mother——did you ever show me the finer things?"

Their angry voices seemed to beat against the noise of the wind and the singing trees, so that the small girl's mother shivered, and drew her cape around her, and ran as fast as she could to her little house.

There were all the shadows to meet her, but she did not sit among them. She made coffee and a dish of milk toast, and set the toast in the oven to keep hot, and then she stood at the window watching. At last she saw through the darkness what looked like a star low down, and she knew that that star was a lantern, and she ran and opened the door wide.

And her young husband set the lantern down on the threshold, and took her in his arms, and said, "The sight of you is more than food and drink."

When he said that, she knew he had had a hard day, but her heart leaped because she knew that what he had said of her was true.

❖

Then they went into the house together, and she set the food before him. And that he might forget his hard day, she told him of her own. And when she came to the part about the next-door-neighbor and the rent, she said, "I am telling you this because it has a happy ending."

And he put his hands over hers and said, "Everything with you has a happy ending."

"Well, this is a happy ending," said the small girl's mother, with all the sapphires in her eyes emphasizing it. "Because when I went over to pay the rent, I was feeling how poor we were and wishing that I had a pink doll for Baby, and books for you, and, and—and a magic carpet to carry us away from work and worry. And then I went into the parlor and saw the tree— with everything hanging on it that was glittering and gorgeous, and then I came home." Her breath was quick and her lips smiling. "I came home—and I was glad I lived in my little home."

"What made you glad, dearest?"

"Oh, love is here; and hate is there, and a boy's deceit, and a man's injustice. They were saying sharp things to each other—and—and—their dinner will be a stalled ox—and in my little house is the faith of a child in the goodness of God, and the bravery of a man who fought for his country—"

She was in his arms now.

176

❖

"And the blessing of a woman who has never known defeat." His voice broke on the words.

In that moment it seemed as if the wind stopped blowing, and as if the trees stopped sighing, as if there was the sound of heavenly singing.

The small girl's mother and the small girl's father sat up very late that night. They popped a great bowlful of crisp snowy corn and made it into balls; they boiled sugar and molasses, and cracked nuts, and made candy of them. They cut funny little Christmas fairies out of paper and painted their jackets bright red, with round silver buttons of the tinfoil that came on cream cheese. And then they put the balls and the candy and the painted fairies and a long red candle in a big basket, and set it away. And the small girl's mother brought out the chocolate mouse.

"We will put this on the clock," she said, "where her eyes will rest on it the first thing in the morning."

So they put it there, and it seemed as natural as life, so that Pussy-purr-up positively licked his chops and sat in front of the clock as if to keep his eye on the chocolate mouse. The small girl's mother said, "She was lovely about giving up the doll, and she will love the tree."

"We'll have to get up very early," said the small girl's father.

"And you'll have to run ahead to light the candle."

Well, they got up before dawn the next morning, and so did the boy-next-door. He was there on the step, waiting, blowing on his hands and beating them quite like the poor little boys do in a Christmas story, who haven't any mittens. But he wasn't a poor little boy, and he had so many pairs of fur-trimmed gloves that he didn't know what to do with them, but he had left the house in such a hurry that he had forgotten to put them on. So there he stood on the front step of the little house, blowing on his hands and beating them. And it was dark, with a sort of pale shine in the heavens, which didn't seem to come from the stars or the herald of the dawn; it was just a mystical silver glow that set the boy's heart to beating.

He had never been out alone like this. He had always stayed in his warm bed until somebody called him, and then he had waited until they had called again, and then he had dressed and gone to breakfast, where his father scolded because he was late, and his mother scolded because he ate too fast. But this day had begun with adventure, and for the first time, under that silvery sky, he felt the thrill of it.

Then suddenly someone came around the

house—someone tall and thin, with a cap on his head and an empty basket in his hands.

"Hello," he said. "A merry Christmas!"

It was the small girl's father, and he put the key in the lock and went in, and turned on a light, and there was the table set for four.

And the small girl's father said, "You see, we have set a place for you. We must eat something before we go out."

And the boy said, "Are we going out? I came to see the tree."

"We are going out to see the tree."

Before the boy could ask any questions, the small girl's mother appeared with fingers on her lips and said, "Sh-sh," and then she began to recite in a hushed voice, "Hickory-Dickory-Dock—"

Then there was a little cry and the sound of dancing feet, and the small girl in a red dressing gown came flying in.

"Oh, Mother, Mother, the mouse is on the clock—the mouse is on the clock!"

Well, it seemed to the little boy that he had never seen anything so exciting as the things that followed. The chocolate mouse went up the clock and under the chair and would have had its tail cut off except that the small girl begged to save it.

❖

"I want to keep it as it is, Mother."

And playing this game as if it were the most important thing in the whole wide world were the small girl's mother and the small girl's father, all laughing and flushed, and chanting the quaint old words to the quaint old music. The boy-next-door held his breath for fear he would wake up from this entrancing dream and find himself in his own big house, alone in his puffy bed, or eating breakfast with his stodgy parents who had never played with him in his life. He found himself laughing too, and flushed and happy, and trying to sing in his funny boy's voice.

The small girl absolutely refused to eat the mouse. "He's my darling Christmas mouse, Mother."

So her mother said, "Well, I'll put him on the clock again, where Pussy-purr-up can't get him while we are out."

"Oh, are we going out?" said the small girl, round-eyed.

"Yes."

"Where are we going?"

"To find Christmas."

That was all the small girl's mother would tell. So they had breakfast, and everything tasted perfectly delicious to the boy-next-door. But first they bowed their heads, and the small girl's father said, "Dear Christ-Child, on this Christmas morning, bless these children, and keep our hearts young and full of love for Thee."

The boy-next-door, when he lifted his head, had a funny feeling as if he wanted to cry, and yet it was a lovely feeling, all warm and comfortable inside.

For breakfast they each had a great baked apple, and great slices of sweet bread and butter, and great glasses of milk, and as soon as they had finished, away they went out of the door and down into the woods back of the house, and when they were deep into the woods, the small girl's father took out of his pocket a little flute and began to play; he played thin piping tunes that went flitting around among the trees, and the small girl and her mother hummed the tunes until it sounded like singing bees, and their feet fairly danced and the boy found himself humming and dancing with them.

Then suddenly the piping ceased, and a hush fell over the wood. It was so still that they could almost hear each other breathe—so still that when a light flamed suddenly in that open space, it burned without a flicker.

The light came from a red candle that was set in the top of a small living tree. It was the only light on the tree, but it showed the snowy balls, and the small red fairies whose coats had silver buttons.

"It's our tree, my darling," he heard the small girl's mother saying.

Suddenly it seemed to the boy that his heart would burst in his breast. He wanted someone to speak to him like that. The small girl sat high on her father's shoulder, and her father held her mother's hand. It was like a chain of gold, their holding hands like that, the loving each other.

The boy reached out and touched the woman's hand. She looked down at him and drew him close. He felt warmed and comforted. Their candle burning there in the darkness was like some sacred fire of friendship. He wished that it would never go out, that he might stand there watching it, with his small cold hand in the clasp of the small girl's mother's hand.

It was late when the boy-next-door got back to his own big house. But he had not been missed. Everybody was up, and everything was upset. The daughter-in-law had declared the night before that she would not stay another day beneath that roof, and off she had gone with her young husband, and her little girl, who was to have had the pink doll on the tree.

❖

"And good riddance," said the next-door-neighbor. But she ate no breakfast, and she went to the kitchen and worked with her maids to get the dinner ready, and there were covers laid for nine instead of 12.

And the next-door-neighbor kept saying, "Good riddance—good riddance," and not once did she say, "A merry Christmas."

But the boy-next-door had something in his heart that was warm and glowing like the candle in the forest, and he came to his mother and said, "May I have the pink dolly?"

She spoke frowningly. "What does a boy want of a doll?"

"I'd like to give it to the little girl next door."

"Do you think I can buy dolls to give away in charity?"

"Well, they gave me a Christmas present."

"What did they give you?"

He opened his hand and showed a little flute tied with a gay red ribbon. He lifted it to his lips and blew on it, a thin piping tune.

"Oh, that," said his mother scornfully. "Why, that's nothing but a reed from the pond."

But the boy knew it was more than that. It was a magic pipe that made you dance, and made your heart warm and happy.

So he said again, "I'd like to give her the doll."
And he reached out his little hand and touched his
mother's—and his eyes were wistful.

His mother's own eyes softened—she had lost
one son that day—and she said, "Oh, well, do as you
please," and went back to the kitchen.

The boy-next-door ran into the great room and
took the doll from the tree, and wrapped her in paper,
and flew out the door and down the brick walk and
straight to the little house. When the door was opened,
he saw that his friends were just sitting down to dinner—and there was the pie, all brown and piping hot,
with a wreath of holly, and the small girl was saying,
"And the onions were silver, and the carrots were
gold—"

The boy-next-door went up to the small girl and
said, "I've brought you a present."

With his eyes all lighted up, he took off the paper in which it was wrapped, and there was the doll, in
rosy frills, with eyes that opened and shut, and shoes
and stockings, and curly hair that was bobbed and
beautiful.

And the small girl, in a whirlwind of happiness,
said, "Is it really my doll?" And the boy-next-door felt
very shy and happy, and he said, "Yes."

And the small girl's mother said, "It was a beau-

184

tiful thing to do," and she bent and kissed him. Again that bursting feeling came into the boy's heart and he lifted his face to hers and said, "May I come sometimes and be your boy?"

And she said, "Yes."

And when at last he went away, she stood in the door and watched him, such a little lad, who knew so little of loving. And because she knew so much of love, her eyes filled to overflowing.

But presently she wiped the tears away and went back to the table; and she smiled at the small girl and at the small girl's father.

"And the potatoes were ivory," she said. "Oh, who would ask for turkey, when they can have pie like this?"

A Full House

MADELEINE L'ENGLE

It was Christmas . . . family time. And the Austin house was full: with a husband, a wife, four children, a grandfather, three dogs, and two cats. There was no more room—nevertheless, along came Evie, along came Eugenia, along came state troopers, along came Maria and Pepita.

Yet in spite of it . . . or because of it . . . it was a Christmas Eve to remember.

(Madeleine L'Engle [1918—   ]

is recognized around the world as one of the finest writers of our time, having successfully published plays, poems, essays, autobiography, and fiction for both children and adults. Perhaps best known is her Time Fantasy Series of children's books, A Wrinkle in Time, A Wind in the Door, A Swiftly Tilting Planet, *and* Many Waters, *books that embody her unique blend of science fiction, family love, and moral responsibility.* A Wrinkle in Time *won the Newbery Medal in 1963, the Lewis Carroll Shelf Award in 1965, and was runner up for the Hans Christian Andersen Award in 1964. She also wrote a series of books based on her family, including* The Twenty-four Days Before Christmas: An Austin Family Story. *A practicing Christian, religion is crucial in all her writings.)*

To anybody who lives in a city or even a sizable town, it may not sound like much to be the director of a volunteer choir in a postcard church in a postcard village, but I was the choir director and largely responsible for the Christmas Eve service, so it was very much of a much for me. I settled my four children and my father, who was with us for Christmas, in a front pew and went up to the stuffy choir-robing room. I was missing my best baritone, my husband, Wally, because he had been called to the hospital. He's a country doctor, and I'm used to his pocket beeper going off during the church service. I missed him, of course, but I knew he'd been called to deliver a baby, and a Christmas baby is always a joy.

The service went beautifully. Nobody flatted, and Eugenia Underhill, my lead soprano, managed for once not to breathe in the middle of a word. The only near disaster came when she reached for the high C in "O Holy Night," hit it brilliantly—and then down fell her upper plate. Eugenia took it in good stride, pushed her teeth back in place and finished her solo. When she sat down, she doubled over with mirth.

The church looked lovely, lighted entirely by candlelight, with pine boughs and holly banking the windows. The Christmas Eve service is almost entirely music, hence my concern; there is never a sermon, but our minister reads excerpts from the Christmas sermons of John Donne and Martin Luther.

When the dismissal and blessings were over, I heaved a sigh of relief. Now I could attend to our own Christmas at home. I collected my family, and we went out into the night. A soft, feathery snow was beginning to fall. People called out "Goodnight" and "Merry Christmas." I was happily tired, and ready for some peace and quiet for the rest of the evening—our service is over by nine.

I hitched Rob, my sleeping youngest, from one hip to the other. The two girls, Vicky and Suzy, walked on either side of their grandfather; John, my eldest, was with me. They had all promised to go to bed without protest as soon as we had finished all our traditional Christmas rituals. We seem to add new ones each year so that Christmas Eve bedtime gets later and later.

I piled the kids into the station wagon, thrusting Rob into John's arms. Father and I got in the front, and I drove off into the snow, which was falling more heavily. I hoped that it would not be a blizzard and that Wally would get home before the roads got too bad.

Our house is on the crest of a hill, a mile out of the village. As I looked uphill, I could see the lights of our outdoor Christmas tree twinkling warmly through the snow. I turned up our back road, feeling suddenly very tired. When I drove up to the garage and saw that Wally's car was not there, I tried not to let Father or the children see my disappointment. I began ejecting the kids from the back. It was my father who first noticed what looked like a bundle of clothes by the storm door.

"Victoria," he called to me. "What's this?"

The bundle of clothes moved. A tear-stained face emerged, and I recognized Evie, who had moved from the village with her parents two years ago, when she was 16. She had been our favorite and most loyal babysitter, and we all missed her. I hadn't seen her—or heard anything about her—in all this time.

"Evie!" I cried. "What is it? What's the matter?"

She moved stiffly, as though she had been huddled there in the cold for a long time. Then she held her arms out to me in a childlike gesture. "Mrs. Austin—" She sighed as I bent down to kiss her. And then, "Mom threw me out. So I came here." She dropped the words simply, as though she had no doubt that she would find a welcome in our home. She had on a shapeless, inadequate coat, and a bare toe stuck through a hole in one of her sneakers.

I put my arms around her and helped her up. "Come in. You must be frozen."

The children were delighted to see Evie and crowded around, hugging her, so it was a few minutes before we got into the kitchen and past the dogs who were loudly welcoming us home. There were Mr. Rochester, our Great Dane; Colette, a silver-gray

❖

French poodle who bossed the big dog unmercifully; and, visiting us for the Christmas holidays while his owners were on vacation, a 10-month-old Manchester terrier named Guardian. Daffodil, our fluffy amber cat, jumped on top of the bridge to get out of the way, and Prune Whip, our black-and-white cat, skittered across the floor and into the living room.

The kids turned on lights all over downstairs, and John called, "Can I turn on the Christmas-tree lights?"

I turned again to Evie, who simply stood in the middle of the big kitchen-dining room, not moving. "Evie, welcome. I'm sorry it's such chaos—let me take your coat." At first she resisted and then let me slip the worn material off her shoulders. Under the coat she wore a sweater and a plaid skirt; the skirt did not button, but was fastened with a pin, and for an obvious reason: Evie was not about to produce another Christmas baby, but she was very definitely pregnant.

Her eyes followed mine. Rather defiantly, she said, "That's why I'm here."

I thought of Evie's indifferent parents, and I thought about Christmas Eve. I put my arm around her for a gentle hug. "Tell me about it."

"Do I have to?"

"I think it might help, Evie."

Suzy, 8 years old and still young enough to pull at my skirt and be whiny when she was tired, now did just that to get my full attention. "Let's put out the cookies and cocoa for Santa Claus *now*."

Suddenly there was an anguished shout from the living room. "Come quick!" John yelled, and I went running.

Guardian was sitting under the tree, a long piece of green ribbon hanging from his mouth. Around him was a pile of Christmas wrappings, all nicely chewed. While we were in church, our visiting dog had unwrapped almost every single package under the tree.

Vicky said, "But we won't know who anything came from . . ."

Suzy burst into tears. "That dog has ruined it all!"

Evie followed us in. She was carrying Rob, who was sleeping with his head down on her shoulder. Father looked at her with his special warm glance that took in and assessed any situation. "Sit down, Evie," he ordered.

I took Rob from her, and when she had more or less collapsed in Wally's special chair in front of the big fireplace, he asked, "When did you eat last?"

"I don't know. Yesterday, I think."

I dumped my sleeping child on the sofa and then headed for the kitchen, calling, "Vicky, Suzy, come help me make sandwiches. I'll warm up some soup. John, make up the couch in Daddy's office for Evie, please."

Our house is a typical square New England farmhouse. Upstairs are four bedrooms. Downstairs we have a big, rambling kitchen-dining room, all unexpected angles and nooks; a large, L-shaped living room and my husband's office, which he uses two nights a week for his patients in the nearby village. As I took a big jar of vegetable soup from the refrigerator and poured a good helping into a saucepan, I could hear my father's and Evie's voices, low, quiet, and I wondered if Evie was pouring out her story to him. I remembered hearing that her father seldom came home without stopping first at the tavern and that her mother had the reputation of being no better than she should be. And yet I knew that their response to Evie's pregnancy would be one of righteous moral indignation. To my daughters I said, "There's some egg salad in the fridge. Make a big sandwich for Evie."

I lifted the curtains and looked out the window. The roads would soon be impassable. I wanted my husband to be with us, in the warmth and comfort of our home.

I went back to the stove and poured a bowl of

soup for Evie. Vicky and Suzy had produced a messy but edible sandwich and then gone off. I called Evie, and she sat at the table and began to eat hungrily. I sat beside her. "How did it happen? Do I know him?"

She shook her head. "No. His name's Billy. After we left here, I didn't feel—I didn't feel that anybody in the world loved me. I think that Mom and Pop are always happiest when I'm out of the house. When I was baby-sitting for you, I thought I saw what love was like. Mrs. Austin, I was lonely, I was so lonely it hurt. Then I met Billy, and I thought he loved me. So when he wanted to—I—but then I found out that it didn't have anything to do with love, at least not for Billy. When I got pregnant, he said, well, how did I even know it was his? Mrs. Austin, I never, never was with anyone else. When he said that, I know it was his way of telling me to get out, just like Mom and Pop."

The girls had wandered back into the kitchen while we were talking, and Suzy jogged at my elbow. "Why does Evie's tummy look so big?"

The phone rang. I called, "John, get it please."

In a moment he came into the kitchen, looking slightly baffled. "It was someone from the hospital saying Dad's on his way home, and would we please make up the bed in the waiting room."

Evie looked up from her soup. "Mrs. Austin——"

she turned her frightened face toward me, fearful, no doubt, that we were going to put her out.

"It's all right, Evie." I was thinking quickly. "John, would you mind sleeping in the guest room with Grandfather?"

"If Grandfather doesn't mind."

My father called from the living room, "Grandfather would enjoy John's company."

"All right then, Evie." I poured more soup into her bowl. "You can sleep in John's bed. Rob will love sharing his room with you."

"But who is Daddy bringing home?" John asked.

"What's wrong with Evie's tummy?" Suzy persisted.

"And why didn't Daddy tell us?" Vicky asked.

"Tell us what?" Suzy demanded.

"Who he's bringing home with him!" John said.

Evie continued to spoon the soup into her mouth, at the same time struggling not to cry. I put one hand on her shoulder, and she reached up for it, asking softly, as the girls and John went into the living room, "Mrs. Austin, I knew you wouldn't turn me away on Christmas Eve, but what about . . . well, may I stay with you for a little while? I have some thinking to do."

"Of course you can, and you do have a lot of thinking to do—the future of your baby, for instance."

"I know. Now that it's getting so close, I'm beginning to get really scared. At first I thought I wanted the baby, I thought it would make Billy and me closer, make us a family like you and Dr. Austin and your kids, but now I know that was just wishful thinking. Sometimes I wish I could go back, be your baby-sitter again . . . Mrs. Austin, I just don't know what I'm going to do with a baby of my own."

I pressed her hand. "Evie, I know how you feel, but things have a way of working out. Try to stop worrying, at least tonight—it's Christmas Eve."

"And I'm home," Evie said. "I feel more at home in this house than anywhere else."

I thought of my own children and hoped that they would never have cause to say that about someone else's house. To Evie I said, "Relax then, and enjoy Christmas. The decisions don't have to be made tonight."

My father ambled into the kitchen, followed by the three dogs. "I think the dogs are telling me they need to go out," he said. "I'll just walk around the house with them and see what the night is doing." He opened the kitchen door and let the dogs precede him.

I opened the curtains, not only to watch the

progress of my father and the dogs, but to give myself a chance to think about Evie and how we could help her. More was needed, I knew, than just a few days' shelter. She had no money, no home, and a baby was on the way. . . . No wonder she looked scared—and trapped. I watched the falling snow and longed to hear the sound of my husband's car. Like Vicky, I wondered who on earth he was bringing home with him. Then I saw headlights coming up the road and heard a car slowing down, but the sound was not the slightly bronchial purr of Wally's car. Before I had a chance to wonder who it could be, the phone rang. "I'll get it!" Suzy yelled, and ran, beating Vicky. "Mother, it's Mrs. Underhill."

I went to the phone. Eugenia's voice came happily over the line. "Wasn't the Christmas Eve service beautiful! And did you see my teeth?" She laughed.

"You sang superbly, anyhow."

"Listen, why I called—and you have two ovens, don't you?"

"Yes."

"Something's happened to mine. The burners work, but the oven is dead, and there's no way I can get anyone to fix it now. So what I wondered is, can I cook my turkey in one of your ovens?"

"Sure," I said, though I'd expected to use the second oven for the creamed-onion casserole and sweet potatoes—but how could I say no to Eugenia?

"Can I come over with my turkey now?" she asked. "I like to put it in a slow oven Christmas Eve, the way you taught me. Then I won't have to bother you again tomorrow."

"Sure, Eugenia, come on over, but drive carefully."

"I will. Thanks," she said.

John murmured, "Just a typical Christmas Eve at the Austins," as the kitchen door opened, and my father and the dogs came bursting in, followed by a uniformed state trooper.

When Evie saw him, she looked scared.

My father introduced the trooper, who turned to me. "Mrs. Austin, I've been talking with your father here, and I think we've more or less sorted things out." Then he looked at Evie. "Young lady, we've been looking for you. We want to talk to you about your friends."

The color drained from her face.

"Don't be afraid," the trooper reassured her. "We just want to know where we can find you. I understand that you'll be staying with the Austins for a while—for the next few weeks, at least." He looked at my father, who nodded, and I wondered what the two had said to each other. Was Evie in more trouble than I thought?

She murmured something inaudible, keeping her eyes fastened to her soup.

"Well, now, it's Christmas Eve," the trooper said, "and I'd like to be getting on home. It's bedtime for us all."

"We're waiting for Daddy," Suzy said. "He's on his way home."

"And he's bringing someone with him," Vicky added.

"Looks like you've got a full house," the trooper said. "Well, 'night, folks."

My father showed him out, then shut the door behind him.

"What was that—" John started to ask.

I quickly said, "What I want all of you to do is to go upstairs, right now, and get ready for bed. That's an order."

"But what about Daddy—"

"And whoever he's bringing—"

"And reading 'The Night Before Christmas' and Saint Luke—"

"And you haven't sung to us—"

I spoke through the clamor. "Upstairs. Now. You

200

can come back down as soon as you're all ready for bed."

Evie rose. "Shall I get Rob?" I had the feeling she wanted to get away, escape my questions.

"We might as well leave him. Vicky, get Evie some nightclothes from my closet, please."

When they had all finally trooped upstairs, including Evie, I turned to my father who was perched on a stool by the kitchen counter. "All right, Dad, tell me about it," I said. "What did the officer tell you?"

"That soup smells mighty good," he said. I filled a bowl for him and waited.

Finally he said, "Evie was going with a bunch of kids who weren't much good. A couple of them were on drugs—not Evie, fortunately, or her boyfriend. And they stole some cars, just for kicks, and then abandoned them. The police are pretty sure that Evie wasn't involved, but they want to talk to her and her friends, and they've been trying to round them up. They went to her parents' house looking for her. Her mother and father made it seem as if she'd run away—they didn't mention that they'd put her out. All they did was denounce her, but they did suggest she might have come here."

"Poor Evie. There's so much good in her, and sometimes I wonder how, with her background. What did you tell the trooper?"

"I told him Evie was going to stay with you and Wally for the time being, that you would take responsibility for her. They still want to talk to her, but I convinced him to wait until after Christmas. I guess the trooper figured that, as long as she's with you, she would be looked after and out of harm's way."

"Thank goodness. All she needs is to be hauled into a station house on Christmas Eve—" Just then the heavy knocker on the kitchen door banged.

It was Eugenia, with a large turkey in a roasting pan in her arms. "I'll just pop it in the oven," she said. "If you think about basting it when you baste yours, OK, but it'll do all right by itself. Hey, you don't have yours in yet!"

What with one thing and another, I'd forgotten our turkey, but it was prepared and ready in the cold pantry. I whipped out and brought it in and put it in the other oven.

As Eugenia drove off, the dogs started with their welcoming bark, and I heard the sound of Wally's engine.

The children heard, too, and came rushing downstairs. "Wait!" I ordered. "Don't mob Daddy. And remember he has someone with him."

Evie came slowly downstairs, wrapped in an old

blue plaid robe of mine. John opened the kitchen door, and the dogs went galloping out.

"Whoa! Down!" I could hear my husband command. And then, to the children, "Make way!" The children scattered, and Wally came in, his arm around a young woman whom I had never seen before. She was holding a baby in her arms.

"This is Maria Heraldo," Wally said. "Maria, my wife, Victoria. And——" He looked at the infant.

"Pepita," she said, "after her father."

Wally took the baby. "Take off your coat," he said to the mother. "Maria's husband was killed in an accident at work two weeks ago. Her family are all in South America, and she was due to be released from the hospital today. Christmas Eve didn't seem to me to be a very good time for her to be alone."

I looked at the baby, who had an amazing head of dark hair. "She isn't the baby——"

"That I delivered tonight? No, though that little boy was slow in coming—that's why we're so late." He smiled down at the young woman. "Pepita was born a week ago." He looked up and saw our children hovering in the doorway, Evie and my father behind them. When he saw Evie, he raised his eyebrows in a questioning gesture.

"Evie's going to be staying with us for a while," I told him. Explanations would come later. "Maria, would you like some soup?"

"I would," my husband said, "and Maria will have some, too." He glanced at the children. "Vicky and Suzy, will you go up to the attic, please, and bring down the cradle?"

They were off like a flash.

My husband questioned the young mother. "Tired?"

"No. I slept while the little boy was being delivered. So did Pepita." And she looked with radiant pride at her daughter who was sleeping again.

"Then let's all go into the living room and warm ourselves in front of the fire. We have some Christmas traditions you might like to share with us."

The young woman gazed up at him, at me, "I'm so grateful to you——"

"Nonsense. Come along."

Then Maria saw Evie, and I watched her eyes flick to Evie's belly, then upward, and the two young women exchanged a long look. Evie's glance shifted to the sleeping child, and then she held out her arms. Maria gently handed her the baby, and Evie took the child and cradled it in her arms. For the first time that evening a look of peace seemed to settle over her features.

It is not easy for a woman to raise a child alone, and Maria would probably go back to her family. In any case, her child had obviously been conceived in love, and even death could not take that away. Evie's eyes were full of tears as she carried Pepita into the living room, but she no longer looked so lost and afraid, and I had the feeling that whatever happened, Evie would be able to handle it. She would have our help—Wally's and mine—for as long as she needed it, but something told me that she wouldn't need it for long.

In a short while, Maria was ensconced in one of the big chairs, a bowl of soup on the table beside her. Evie put the baby in the cradle, and knelt, rocking it gently. Wally sat on the small sofa with Rob in his lap, a mug of soup in one hand. The two girls were curled up on the big davenport, one on either side of their grandfather, who had his arms around them. I sat across from Maria, and Evie came and sat on the footstool by me. John was on the floor in front of the fire. The only light was from the Christmas tree and the flickering flames of the fire. On the mantel were a cup of cocoa and a plate of cookies.

"Now," my husband said, " 'Twas the night before Christmas, when all through the house . . .' "

When he had finished, with much applause from

the children and Evie and Maria, he looked to me. "Your turn."

John jumped up and handed me my guitar. I played and sang, "I Wonder as I Wander," and then "In the Bleak Mid-winter," and ended up with "Let All Mortal Flesh Keep Silence." As I put the guitar away, I saw Maria reach out for Evie, and the two of them briefly clasped hands.

"And now," Wally said, "your turn, please, Grandfather."

My father opened his Bible and began to read. When he came to "And she brought forth her firstborn son, and wrapped him in swaddling clothes, and laid him in a manger; because there was no room for them in the inn," I looked at Maria, who was rocking the cradle with her foot while her baby murmured in her sleep. Evie, barely turning, keeping her eyes fastened on the sleeping infant, leaned her head against my knee, rubbing her cheek against the wool of my skirt.

Suzy was sleeping with her head down in her grandfather's lap, while he continued to read: "And suddenly there was with the angel a multitude of the heavenly host praising God, and saying, Glory to God in the highest, and on earth peace, good will toward men."

I remembered John saying, "Just a typical Christmas Eve at the Austins," and I wondered if there ever could be such a thing as a typical Christmas. For me, each one is unique. This year our house was blessed by Evie and her unborn child, by Eugenia's feeling free to come and put her turkey in our stove, and by Maria and Pepita turning our plain New England farmhouse into a stable.

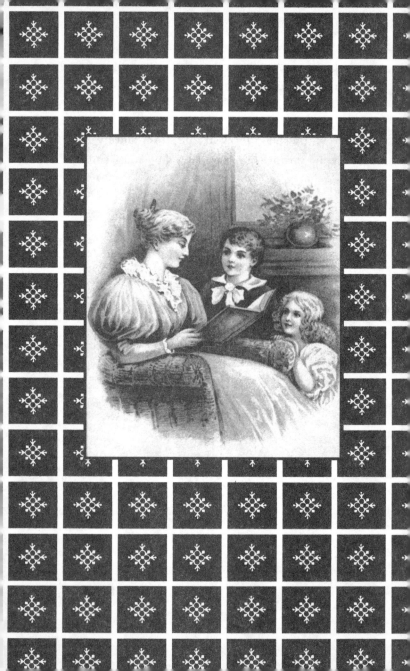

My Christmas Miracle

TAYLOR CALDWELL

So famous and renowned is Taylor Caldwell to us today that it is difficult for us to conceptualize her as a wan, depressed, and frightened young mother; alone, nearly destitute, jobless, and having to face the bleakest Christmas of her life. She had almost lost faith in God Himself.

And then . . .

For many of us, one Christmas stands out from all the others, the one when the meaning of the day shone clearest.

Although I did not guess it, my own "truest" Christmas began on a rainy spring day in the bleakest year of my life. Recently divorced, I was in my 20s, had no job, and was on my way downtown to go the rounds of the employment offices. I had no umbrella, for my old one had fallen apart, and I could not afford another one. I sat down in the streetcar, and there against the seat was a beautiful silk umbrella with a silver handle inlaid with gold and flecks of bright enamel. I had never seen anything so lovely.

I examined the handle and saw a name engraved among the golden scrolls. The usual procedure would have been to turn in the umbrella to the conductor, but on impulse, I decided to take it with me and find the owner myself. I got off the streetcar in a downpour and thankfully opened the umbrella to protect myself. Then I searched a telephone book for the name on the umbrella and found it. I called, and a lady answered.

Yes, she said in surprise, that was her umbrella, which her parents, now dead, had given her for a birthday present. But, she added, it had been stolen from her locker at school (she was a teacher) more than a year before. She was so excited that I forgot I was look-

❖

ing for a job and went directly to her small house. She took the umbrella, and her eyes filled with tears.

The teacher wanted to give me a reward, but—though $20 was all I had in the world—her happiness at retrieving this special possession was such that to have accepted money would have spoiled something. We talked for a while, and I must have given her my address. I don't remember.

The next six months were wretched. I was able to obtain only temporary employment here and there, for a small salary, though this was what they now call the Roaring Twenties. But I put aside 25 or 50 cents when I could afford it for my little girl's Christmas presents. (It took me six months to save $8.) My last job ended the day before Christmas, my $30 rent was soon due, and I had $15 to my name—which Peggy and I would need for food. She was home from her convent boarding school and was excitedly looking forward to her gifts the next day, which I had already purchased. I had bought her a small tree, and we were going to decorate it that night.

The stormy air was full of the sound of Christmas merriment as I walked from the streetcar to my small apartment. Bells rang and children shouted in the bitter dusk of the evening, and windows were lighted and everyone was running and laughing. But there would be no Christmas for me, I knew, no gifts, no remembrance whatsoever. As I struggled through the snowdrifts, I just about reached the lowest point in my life. Unless a miracle happened I would be homeless in January, foodless, jobless. I had prayed steadily for weeks, and there had been no answer but this coldness and darkness, this harsh air, this abandonment. God and men had completely forgotten me. I felt old as death, and as lonely. What was to become of us?

I looked in my mailbox. There were only bills in it, a sheaf of them, and two white envelopes which I was sure contained more bills. I went up three dusty flights of stairs, and I cried, shivering in my thin coat. But I made myself smile so I could greet my little daughter with a pretense of happiness. She opened the door for me and threw herself in my arms, screaming joyously and demanding that we decorate the tree immediately.

Peggy was not yet 6 years old, and had been alone all day while I worked. She had set our kitchen table for our evening meal, proudly, and put pans out and the three cans of food which would be our dinner. For some reason, when I looked at those pans and cans, I felt brokenhearted. We would have only hamburgers for our Christmas dinner tomorrow, and gelatin. I stood in the cold little kitchen, and misery overwhelmed me. For the first time in my life, I doubted the existence of God and His mercy, and the coldness in my heart was colder than ice.

The doorbell rang, and Peggy ran fleetly to answer it, calling that it must be Santa Claus. Then I heard a man talking heartily to her and went to the door. He was a delivery man, and his arms were full of big parcels, and he was laughing at my child's frenzied joy and her dancing. "This is a mistake," I said, but he read the name on the parcels, and they were for me. When he had gone I could only stare at the boxes. Peggy and I sat on the floor and opened them. A huge doll, three times the size of the one I had bought for her. Gloves. Candy. A beautiful leather purse. Incredible! I looked for the name of the sender. It was the teacher, the address simply "California," where she had moved.

Our dinner that night was the most delicious I had ever eaten. I could only pray in myself, "Thank you, Father." I forgot I had no money for the rent and only $15 in my purse and no job. My child and I ate and laughed together in happiness. Then we decorated the little tree and marveled at it. I put Peggy to bed and set up her gifts around the tree, and a sweet peace flooded me like a benediction. I had some hope again. I could even examine the sheaf of bills without cringing. Then I opened the two white envelopes. One contained a check for $30 from a company I had worked for briefly in the summer. It was, said a note, my "Christmas bonus." My rent!

The other envelope was an offer of a permanent position with the government—to begin two days after Christmas. I sat with the letter in my hand and the check on the table before me, and I think that was the most joyful moment of my life up to that time.

The church bells began to ring. I hurriedly looked at my child, who was sleeping blissfully, and ran down to the street. Everywhere people were walking to church to celebrate the birth of the Savior. People smiled at me and I smiled back. The storm had stopped, the sky was pure and glittering with stars.

"The Lord is born!" sang the bells to the crystal night and the laughing darkness. Someone began to sing, "Come, all ye faithful!" I joined in and sang with the strangers all about me.

I am not alone at all, I thought. *I was never alone at all.*

And that, of course, is the message of Christmas. We are never alone. Not when the night is darkest, the wind coldest, the world seemingly most indifferent. For this is still the time God chooses.

A Day of
Pleasant Bread

DAVID GRAYSON

When Christmas nears, our thoughts often turn to those less fortunate than we—the poor, the needy, the destitute. But what if there are none in that condition nearby? If so, would one then—perish the thought! —have to resort to inviting the rich?

(Pulitzer Prize winning author Ray Stannard Baker [1870–1946] led a double life. In public he was the renowned editor, journalist, and author of the monumental eight-volume life of Woodrow

Wilson. In private, under the pen name of David Grayson, he was free to roam the country as a homespun philosopher and humorist. In the process, we are all the richer for such books as Adventures in Contentment, Adventures in Friendship, The Friendly Road, Great Possessions, *and* Adventures in Understanding.*)*

They have all gone now, and the house is very still. For the first time this evening I can hear the familiar sound of the December wind blustering about the house, complaining at closed doorways, asking questions at the shutters; but here in my room, under the green reading lamp, it is warm and still. Although Harriet has closed the doors, covered the coals in the fireplace, and said goodnight, the atmosphere still seems to tingle with the electricity of genial humanity.

The parting voice of the Scotch preacher still booms in my ears:

"This," said he, as he was going out of our door, wrapped like an Arctic highlander in cloaks and tippets, "has been a day of pleasant bread."

One of the very pleasantest I can remember!

I sometimes think we expect too much of Christmas Day. We try to crowd into it the long arrears of kindliness and humanity of the whole year. As for me, I like to take my Christmas a little at a time, all through the year. And thus I drift along into the holidays——let them overtake me unexpectedly——waking up some fine morning and suddenly saying to myself:

"Why, this is Christmas Day!"

How the discovery makes one bound out of his bed! What a new sense of life and adventure it imparts! Almost anything may happen on a day like this——one thinks. I may meet friends I have not seen before in years. Who knows? I may discover that this is a far better and kindlier world than I had ever dreamed it could be.

So I sing out to Harriet as I go down:

"Merry Christmas, Harriet"——and not waiting for her sleepy reply, I go down and build the biggest, warmest, friendliest fire of the year. Then I get into my thick coat and mittens and open the back door. All around the sill, deep on the step, and all about the yard lies the drifted snow: it has transformed my wood pile into a grotesque Indian mound, and it frosts the roof of my barn like a wedding cake. I go at it lustily with my wooden shovel, clearing out a pathway to the gate. . . .

All the morning as I went about my chores I had a peculiar sense of expected pleasure. It seemed certain to me that something unusual and adventurous was about to happen——and if it did not happen offhand, why, I was there to make it happen! When I went in to breakfast (do you know the fragrance of broiling bacon when you have worked for an hour before breakfast on a morning of zero weather? If you do not, consider that heaven still has gifts in store for you!)——when I went in to breakfast, I fancied that Harriet looked preoccupied, but I was too busy just then (hot corn muffins) to make an inquiry, and I knew by experience that the best solvent of secrecy is patience.

"David," said Harriet presently, "the cousins can't come!"

"Can't come!" I exclaimed.

"Why, you act as if you were delighted."

"No——well, yes," I said. "I knew that some extraordinary adventure was about to happen!"

"Adventure! It's a cruel disappointment——I was all ready for them."

"Harriet," I said, "adventure is just what we make it. And aren't we to have the Scotch preacher and his wife?"

"But I've got such a *good* dinner."

"Well," I said, "there are no two ways about it: it must be eaten! You may depend upon me to do my duty."

"We'll have to send out into the highways and compel them to come in," said Harriet ruefully.

I had several choice observations I should have liked to make upon this problem, but Harriet was plainly not listening; she sat with her eyes fixed reflectively on the coffeepot. I watched her for a moment, then I remarked:

"There aren't any."

"David," she exclaimed, "how did you know what I was thinking about?"

"I merely wanted to show you," I said, "that my genius is not properly appreciated in my own household. You thought of highways, didn't you? Then you thought of the poor; especially the poor on Christmas Day; then of Mrs. Heney, who isn't poor anymore, having married John Daniels; and then I said 'There aren't any.' "

Harriet laughed.

"It has come to a pretty pass," she said, "when there are no poor people to invite to dinner on Christmas Day."

"It's a tragedy, I'll admit," I said, "but let's be logical about it."

"I am willing," said Harriet, "to be as logical as you like."

"Then," I said, "having no poor to invite to dinner, we must necessarily try the rich. That's logical, isn't it?"

"Who?" asked Harriet, which is just like a woman. Whenever you get a good healthy argument started with her, she will suddenly short-circuit it, and want to know if you mean Mr. Smith, or Joe Perkins's boys, which I maintain is *not* logical.

"Well, there are the Starkweathers," I said.

"David!"

"They're rich, aren't they?"

"Yes, but you know how they live—what dinners they have—and besides, they probably have a houseful of company."

"Weren't you telling me the other day how many people who were really suffering were too proud to let anyone know about it? Weren't you advising the necessity of getting acquainted with people and finding out —tactfully, of course—you made a point of fact— what the trouble was?"

"But I was talking of *poor* people."

"Why shouldn't a rule that is good for poor people be equally as good for rich people? Aren't they proud?"

"Oh, you can argue," observed Harriet.

"And I can act, too," I said. "I am now going over to invite the Starkweathers. I heard a rumor that their cook has left them, and I expect to find them starving in their parlor. Of course they'll be very haughty and proud, but I'll be tactful, and when I go away I'll casually leave a diamond tiara in the front hall."

"What *is* the matter with you this morning?"

"Christmas," I said.

I can't tell how pleased I was with the enterprise I had in mind: it suggested all sort of amusing and surprising developments. Moreover, I left Harriet, finally, in the breeziest of spirits, having quite forgotten her disappointment over the nonarrival of the cousins.

"If you *should* get the Starkweathers——"

" 'In the bright lexicon of youth,' " I observed, " 'there is no such word as fail.' "

So I set off up the town road. A team or two had already been that way and had broken a track through the snow. The sun was now fully up, but the air still tingled with the electricity of zero weather. And the fields! I have seen the fields of June and the fields of October, but I think I never saw our countryside, hills and valleys, tree spaces and brook bottoms, more enchantingly beautiful than it was this morning. Snow everywhere——the fences half hidden, the bridges clogged, the trees laden: where the road was hard it squeaked under my feet, and where it was soft I strode through the drifts. And the air went to one's head like wine!

So I tramped past the Pattersons'. The old man, a grumpy old fellow, was going to the barn with a pail on his arm.

"Merry Christmas," I shouted.

He looked around at me wonderingly and did not reply. At the corners I met the Newton boys so wrapped in tippets that I could see only their eyes and the red ends of their small noses. I passed the Williams's house, where there was a cheerful smoke in the chimney and in the window a green wreath with a lively red bow. And I thought how happy everyone must be on a Christmas morning like this! At the hill bridge whom should I meet but the Scotch preacher himself, God bless him!

"Well, well, David," he exclaimed heartily, "Merry Christmas."

I drew my face down and said solemnly:

"Dr. McAlway, I am on a most serious errand."

"Why, now, what's the matter?" He was all sympathy at once.

"I am out in the highways trying to compel the poor of this neighborhood to come to our feast."

The Scotch preacher observed me with a twinkle in his eye.

"David," he said, putting his hand to his mouth as if to speak in my ear, "there is a poor man you will na' have to compel."

"Oh, you don't count," I said. "You're coming anyhow."

Then I told him of the errand with our millionaire friends, into the spirit of which he entered with the greatest zest. He was full of advice and much excited lest I fail to do a thoroughly competent job. For a moment I think he wanted to take the whole thing out of my hands.

"Man, man, it's a lovely thing to do," he exclaimed, "but I ha' me doots—I ha' me doots."

At parting he hesitated a moment, and with a serious face inquired:

"Is it by any chance a goose?"

"It is," I said, "a goose—a big one."

He heaved a sigh of complete satisfaction. "You have comforted my mind," he said, "with the joys of anticipation—a goose, a big goose."

So I left him and went onward toward the Starkweathers'. Presently I saw the great house standing among its wintry trees. There was smoke in the chimney but no other evidence of life. At the gate my spirits, which had been of the best all the morning, began to fail me. Though Harriet and I were well enough acquainted with the Starkweathers, yet at this late moment on Christmas morning it did seem rather a harebrained scheme to think of inviting them to dinner.

"Never mind," I said, "they'll not be displeased to see me anyway."

I waited in the reception room, which was cold and felt damp. In the parlor beyond I could see the innumerable things of beauty—furniture, pictures, books, so very, very much of everything—with which the room was filled. I saw it now, as I had often seen it before, with a peculiar sense of weariness. How all these things, though beautiful enough in themselves, must clutter up a man's life!

Do you know, the more I look into life, the more things it seems to me I can successfully lack—and continue to grow happier. How many kinds of food I do not need, nor cooks to cook them, how much curious clothing nor tailors to make it, how many books that I never read, and pictures that are not worthwhile! The further I run, the more I feel like casting aside all such impedimenta—lest I fail to arrive at the far goal of my endeavor.

I like to think of an old Japanese nobleman I once read about, who ornamented his house with a single vase at a time, living with it, absorbing its message of beauty, and when he tired of it, replacing it with another. I wonder if he had the right way, and we, with so many objects to hang on our walls, place on our shelves, drape on our chairs, and spread on our floors, have mistaken our course and placed our hearts upon the multiplicity rather than the quality of our possessions!

Presently Mr. Starkweather appeared in the doorway. He wore a velvet smoking jacket and slippers; and somehow, for a bright morning like this, he seemed old, and worn, and cold.

"Well, well, friend," he said, "I'm glad to see you."

He said it as though he meant it.

"Come into the library; it's the only room in the whole house that is comfortably warm. You've no idea what a task it is to heat a place like this in really cold weather. No sooner do I find a man who can run my furnace then he goes off and leaves me."

"I can sympathize with you," I said, "we often have trouble at our house with the man who builds the fires."

He looked around at me quizzically.

"He lies too long in bed in the morning," I said.

❖

By this time we had arrived at the library, where a bright fire was burning in the grate. It was a fine big room, with dark oak furnishings and books in cases along one wall, but this morning it had a disheveled and untidy look. On a little table at one side of the fireplace were the remains of a breakfast; at the other a number of wraps were thrown carelessly upon a chair. As I came in Mrs. Starkweather rose from her place, drawing a silk scarf around her shoulders. She is a robust, rather handsome woman, with many rings on her fingers, and a pair of glasses hanging to a little gold hook on her ample bosom; but this morning she, too, looked worried and old.

"Oh, yes," she said with a rueful laugh, "we're beginning a merry Christmas, as you see. Think of Christmas with no cook in the house!"

I felt as if I had discovered a gold mine. Poor starving millionaires!

But Mrs. Starkweather had not told the whole of her sorrowful story.

"We had a company of friends invited for dinner today," she said, "and our cook was ill—or said she was—and had to go. One of the maids went with her. The man who looks after the furnace disappeared on Friday, and the stableman has been drinking. We can't very well leave the place without someone who is responsible in charge of it——and so here we are. Merry Christmas!"

I couldn't help laughing. Poor people!

"You might," I said, "apply for Mrs. Heney's place."

"Who is Mrs. Heney?" asked Mrs. Starkweather.

"You don't mean to say that you never heard of Mrs. Heney!" I exclaimed. "Mrs. Heney, who is now Mrs. 'Penny' Daniels? You've missed one of our greatest celebrities."

With that, of course, I had to tell them about Mrs. Heney, who has for years performed a most important function in this community. Alone and unaided, she has been the poor whom we are supposed to have always with us. If it had not been for the devoted faithfulness of Mrs. Heney at Thanksgiving, Christmas, and other times of the year, I suppose our Woman's Aid Society and the King's Daughters would have perished miserably of undistributed turkeys and tufted comforters. For years Mrs. Heney filled the place most acceptably. Curbing the natural outpourings of a rather jovial soul, she could upon occasion look as deserving of charity as any person that ever I met. But I pitied the little Heneys: it always comes hard on the children. For weeks after every Thanksgiving and Christmas they always wore a painfully stuffed and suffocated look. I only came to appreciate fully what a self-sacrificing public servant Mrs. Heney really was when I learned that she had taken the desperate alternative of marrying "Penny" Daniels.

"So you think we might possibly aspire to the position?" laughed Mrs. Starkweather.

Upon this I told them of the trouble in our household and asked them to come down and help us enjoy Dr. McAlway and the goose.

When I left, after much more pleasant talk, they both came with me to the door seemingly greatly improved in spirits.

"You've given us something to live for, Mr. Grayson," said Mrs. Starkweather.

So I walked homeward in the highest spirits, and an hour or more later whom should we see in the top of our upper field but Mr. Starkweather and his wife floundering in the snow. They reached the lane literally covered from top to toe with snow and both of them ruddy with the cold.

"We walked over," said Mrs. Starkweather breathlessly, "and I haven't had so much fun in years."

Mr. Starkweather helped her over the fence. The

Scotch preacher stood on the steps to receive them, and we all went in together.

I can't pretend to describe Harriet's dinner: the gorgeous brown goose, and the apple sauce, and all the other things that best go with it, and the pumpkin pie at the end—the finest, thickest, most delicious pumpkin pie I ever ate in all my life. It melted in one's mouth and brought visions of celestial bliss. And I wish I could have a picture of Harriet presiding. I have never seen her happier, or more in her element. Every time she brought in a new dish or took off a cover it was a sort of miracle. And her coffee—but I must not and dare not elaborate.

And what great talk we had afterward!

I've known the Scotch preacher for a long time, but I never saw him in quite such a mood of hilarity. He and Mr. Starkweather told stories of their boyhood—and we laughed, and laughed—Mrs. Starkweather the most of all. Seeing her so often in her carriage, or in the dignity of her home, I didn't think she had so much jollity in her. Finally she discovered Harriet's cabinet organ, and nothing would do but she must sing for us.

"None of the newfangled ones, Clara," cried her husband: some of the old ones we used to know."

❖

So she sat herself down at the organ and threw her head back and began to sing:

"Believe me, if all those endearing young charms,
Which I gaze on so fondly today——"

Mr. Starkweather jumped up and ran over to the organ and joined in with his deep voice. Harriet and I followed. The Scotch preacher's wife nodded in time with the music, and presently I saw the tears in her eyes. As for Dr. McAlway, he sat on the edge of his chair with his hands on his knees and wagged his shaggy head, and before we got through he, too, joined in with his big sonorous voice:

"Thou wouldst still be adored as this moment
thou art——"

Oh, I can't tell you here——it grows late and there's work tomorrow——all the things we did and said. They stayed until it was dark, and when Mrs. Starkweather was ready to go, she took both of Harriet's hands in hers and said with great earnestness:

"I haven't had such a good time at Christmas since I was a little girl. I shall never forget it."

And the dear old Scotch preacher, when Harriet and I had wrapped him up, went out, saying:

"This has been a day of pleasant bread."

It has; it has. I shall not soon forget it. What a lot of kindness and common human nature—childlike simplicity, if you will—there is in people once you get them down together and persuade them that the things they think serious are not serious at all.

Stranger, Come Home

PEARL S. BUCK

No one has ever bridged the vast yawning chasm between East and West more effectively than Nobel prize winner Pearl Buck. Having grown up as a child of two cultures, Buck was able to do what no previous American had ever done: speak from personal experience as well as from knowledge, from the heart as well as from the mind.

So when America fought in the Far East during World War II, the Korean War, and the Vietnam War, Buck was able to apply her insights and sensitivity to the broken lives and broken dreams that these wars left in their wakes.

Very late in her long and illustrious career, Mrs. Buck wrote "Stranger, Come Home," one of the most moving and haunting stories to come out of the Vietnam War.

"Merry Christmas, darling!"

David Alston heard his wife's voice from the edge of sleep and he opened his eyes. Nancy's pretty face, framed in dark curly hair, was bent over him; she was leaning on one elbow, half sitting up in the big double bed.

He yawned mightily and said, "Not you, Peanut! Kids, yes. One groans and takes it. But a man's wife? That's cruelty, especially on Christmas morning!"

Peanut was what he had called her in the days when they went to high school together, here in this little town in the Green Mountains of Vermont, he carrying her books and she skipping along somewhere near his elbow. He was tall and she was slight, dark to his blondness, gay to his gravity. He tried now to remember to call her Nancy in public and in front of the children, but she was Peanut when they were alone. He drew her down to kiss her. She yielded with a nice readiness, drawing back only when she became breathless.

"I couldn't sleep," she said.

"Why not?" he asked wryly. "We didn't get to bed until one in the morning. I thought I'd never get those pedal carts put together—one was bad enough, but three! I knew the boys had to have them this Christmas, but I didn't think Susan would want one, too."

"She wants whatever the boys have . . . David!"

"Yes? What now?"

"Do you think they'll see?"

"See what?"

"You know what I mean."

He sat up and put aside the covers. "Now, Peanut, you know we said we weren't going to worry. We said that from the very beginning—or as soon as we decided what to do about Susan. We said we'd take the chance."

He disappeared into the bathroom and she lay thinking, trying not to feel apprehensive. For this was a Christmas Day not like any other, and the house held a secret unlike any other—a child whose real identity must be hidden forever. Everyone was to believe that

237

Susan was a little half-American waif from Vietnam, her mother a Vietnamese girl, her father a GI. No one was to know, not even if she did have the honey blonde hair, the amber eyes that all the Alstons had. Still, with her Asian face, it might be possible that no one would guess. Perhaps David's younger brother, Richard, didn't even know there had been a child. And yet . . . the child was named Susan; the name was a family name, David's mother's and grandmother's.

Nancy closed her eyes. So much had happened in the past year! Was it possible that only a year ago Sister Angelica's letter had come from the convent in Saigon, telling of the birth of the baby girl named Susan?

"Thu Van would never tell us the name of the father," Sister Angelica wrote. "Only when she was dead did we find his picture, wrapped in white silk. The address was on the back."

Had Thu Van killed herself? Sister Angelica, in her second letter, had said it was possible.

Nancy herself, upon reading the letter, had said so to David. "I think she did."

"Why?" he had demanded.

"Because—if she loved him and knew he was never coming back—"

Nancy was interrupted in her thoughts. The door burst open and her two small sons rushed into the room, still in their pajamas. They stopped at the sight of the half-empty bed. "Where's Daddy?"

"In the bathroom," she said.

They ran to the bathroom door.

"Daddy, it's not fair!" Jimmy shouted.

"You're not supposed to get up first on Christmas!" Ricky added.

David stuck his head out from behind the shower curtain. "Your mother woke me up—you'll have to speak to her!"

"Mommy—you're naughty!" The boys' faces were alive with mischief.

"I know I am," she confessed. "What shall we do with me?"

They paused to consider this, their eyes big. Two adorable little boys, she thought, straight blond hair, amber eyes, Alstons both. Ricky, the younger, had been named for Richard, who was safely home from Vietnam when Ricky was born.

Nancy remembered how silent Richard had been in those days, how difficult, how torn by feelings he never divulged. She and David had been glad when, after months of indecision, he had suddenly decided to marry Miranda. Now, of course—Nancy broke off her thoughts and turned to the door.

"Come, Susan," she said.

❧

The little girl, a year younger than Jimmy, a year older than Ricky, stood hesitating at the open door, her great eyes, exquisitely shaped, the corners lifted, wide and watchful. She came forward slowly, doubtfully. She was a grave child, her perfect little face seldom changing. Nancy put her arm about the slender figure in the pink pajamas.

"Merry Christmas," she said. "Merry Christmas to you and to Jimmy and to Ricky! Merry means happy. We'll all be happy today."

She kissed the little girl's cheek and went on. "Everybody get dressed—yes, yes, I know—" she held up a hand. The two boys, now jumping on the bed and starting a pillow fight, were beginning to protest. Nancy went on. "I know we don't usually get dressed first, but we're all awake, Daddy's nearly ready, and today we must be early because Uncle Richard and Aunt Miranda are coming. We can't be in pajamas when they arrive, can we?"

"Off the bed, boys," David ordered. "You heard your mother!"

The voice of authority, and they ran to obey. Only Susan stood motionless within the circle of Nancy's arm. How much did the child understand? She spoke French, but shyly, her voice very soft.

"Et tu, aussi, ma chérie," Nancy said tenderly.

❖

"Don't use French," David said quickly. "She shouldn't hear anything except English. She's ours now."

"Come with me, Susan," Nancy said. "I'll help you dress." She paused at the door, the child clinging to her hand.

"Will you light the tree, David? We shan't be long. I won't let the boys go downstairs first, because I want Susan to see the tree at the same time. I wonder if she's ever seen a Christmas tree?"

"Who knows?" David said.

"There's so much we don't know," Nancy said.

Downstairs, David lighted the tree, and, while he was waiting for the others, began thinking of all he did know.

Sister Angelica had written voluminous letters, but there was more behind and beyond those letters. David was 10 years older than Richard and, when their parents died in an airplane crash, he had tried to take his father's place.

Because of Richard, David had postponed his own marriage. Somehow he had managed to keep this house going, working at the bank and earning enough to eke out the small inheritance their parents had left them. When at last he had married Nancy it was to this home he had brought her. It was inconceivable that they live elsewhere than in this rambling white frame house with the green shutters, standing on a wide, shaded street, the elm trees today laden with Christmas snow. To such a house, American for 200 years, a little half-Asian child had come home. How strange the times!

David remembered how long and difficult the years before his marriage had been. College and then postgraduate work for his younger brother had taken all he could spare, but Nancy had waited for him in understanding patience. It was obvious that Richard was brilliant, and he wanted to be an international lawyer. After the long years of school and summer training jobs, Richard had been called for military service and sent to Vietnam. Now he had a post in the government in Washington, a beginning for a career that already promised success.

Richard and Miranda had waited, too, for he had come back not wanting to be married at once. Miranda's family had money, her father was a senator, and Richard, always proud, had maintained that he would not marry until he could give her a home and a place in a community where she could be happy. Finally, almost a year and a half ago, the marriage had taken place and it was to all appearances happy.

❖

Then last Christmas the greeting card had come from Thu Van, written in French, addressed only by surname—"Monsieur Alston." David had taken it for granted that it was for himself until he read the card: "At this time of the blessed Noël, Richard, my beloved, I write to tell you I am still alive and always loving you. May the good God bless you, is the wish of my longing heart! I forget never. Your Thu Van."

David knew at once what it meant. Richard had loved a girl in Vietnam. This explained everything, his melancholy when he came home, his silence, his wish to postpone his marriage, everything that made him so different from the vigorous and articulate young man he had always been.

David showed the card to Nancy and on Christmas Day they were still discussing what to do. David had been inclined to send no answer. "Certainly I shall not give this card to Richard," he had said in firm decision this day a year ago. "Richard is just settled in a splendid job," he had told Nancy. "Think what this would do to him if it were known—if he knew what we know!"

Nancy, winding up a toy monkey for Ricky, had looked thoughtful. "I feel sorry for that girl," she said. "I do feel you should write to her and explain that you read the letter, thinking it was for you. You could tell her that your brother is happily married and that you do not think it kind or useful to disturb his life, especially since he is no longer with us but lives in another city. Be honest with her——say you aren't giving her card to him. Otherwise her heart will break when there's no answer from Richard."

In the end, David had followed Nancy's advice and had written Thu Van. An answer came, not from her but from Sister Angelica. It, too, was in French.

"Monsieur," Sister Angelica wrote. "Your esteemed letter has come too late. Thu Van died here in the convent on the afternoon of the day of Noël. She had been very sad after the departure of your brother, and since we love her as a former student we had begged her to come and spend the holiday with us. She brought to us her small daughter, Susan, born four years ago. This is your brother's child.

"When I saw the sadness of Thu Van, I inquired of its cause and she told me that your brother and she had a warm affair of the heart, but that he did not marry her. He does not know of the birth of this child. She preferred not to cause him grief by telling him. He left when she was three months pregnant.

"It is her noble nature not to wish to cause pain. Her position became difficult, however, since her family is a well-known one. She was no ordinary prostitute,

❖

but a young woman of dignity as well as great beauty who met your brother, then a young officer, in the home of a French friend. It seems they fell in love immediately and at once the situation became passionate.

"To continue, she spent Noël with us here at the convent, keeping the child beside her all day. After the little one was put to bed, it is said by some that she took one of those swift and subtle poisons that people of the East know so well how to use. Since she was Catholic, I doubt her capable of such sin. But perhaps! At any rate, the child's crying in the morning woke us early, and since it continued we went into the room and found the young mother lying on her pallet, dead.

"It remains now the question of what to do with the child. Is it possible the father would wish to claim her? Since he has a wife, it may be that they would accept this child, and bring her up as their own. She inherits her mother's beauty and something also from her father. Her hair is light in color, her eyes are also light. She is of superior intelligence, as are most of these mixed children, we find. Instruct me, if you please, Monsieur, and I am your obedient servant."

David had handed the letter to Nancy and she read it in silence. They had no chance to talk until that night when the children were in bed, and then they were too tired to talk, too exhausted within by the emotions that all day they had not been able to share in the presence of others. But in the night, Nancy had awakened him.

"David!"

"Yes?"

"I can't sleep."

He had reached for the light, but she had stopped him.

"David!"

"Yes, my love?"

"We must take Susan," Nancy said firmly. "We must take her for our own."

How well he remembered her clear soft voice coming out of the night, there beside him!

"She belongs to our family," Nancy had said.

"I suppose there are thousands of such children," he had said uncertainly. "They can't all be brought here. Perhaps she'd better stay there in the convent. We could send money."

"I'd never be able to sleep again, thinking of her," Nancy said.

Difficulties rose to David's mind. "She may look like Richard," he demurred. "One thing is clear in my mind, Nancy. I won't have Richard's life and career destroyed simply because of a half-Vietnamese child— even though she's his."

Nancy had removed herself from his arms abruptly when he finished. "I think of her as half American," she said clearly, "and therefore half ours. And her mother is dead. She killed herself because she loved your brother hopelessly. And he did love her in some fashion because he let her love him. There's an obligation. And the letter says that in Asia the child belongs to the father. The father is your brother."

The upshot of her determination was that they had begun the long process of adopting Susan, not as Richard's child but as a waif, the child of an anonymous American soldier in Vietnam who might have been any soldier but whose mother, a Vietnamese lady, now dead, had left her in a convent.

The agency social worker had been doubtful and reluctant. "We must first see if we can find a Catholic family for this child of a Catholic," she had said.

They had gone through the long ordeal of waiting until in the end it was proved there was no Catholic family who wanted the child, at least within the area of the agency, and reluctantly Susan was given to them. It had taken a year shorter by one week, and so one week ago Susan had arrived at the airport in New York, and they had gone to meet her, he and Nancy. Susan had descended from the plane, the stewardess holding her hand, looking lost and tearful. Nancy had opened her arms then and the little girl had gone straight into that haven.

"I've always wanted a daughter," Nancy had said through her tears.

The door opened softly at this moment and David saw Susan standing there. She had come downstairs alone. It was the first act of her own volition. Until now she had stayed where she was put, followed where she was led. Here she stood, transfixed at the sight of the glittering tree. Nancy had bought her a red velvet dress with a wide white collar and had put it on her this morning. Above it her great eyes shone luminous and lit from within, and her straight blonde hair hung to her shoulders. She came nearer to the tree, softly on tiptoe, and then gazed at it, her finger on her lip.

"Jolie," she whispered. *"Très, très jolie!"*

He watched her in fascination, surely the loveliest child ever born. He felt a foolish dart of jealousy that Richard was the father.

"Pretty," he said gently, "very, very pretty."

She turned her grave eyes to his face. "Pret-ty," she echoed. She had not allowed him to take her hand or lift her to his knee, clinging always to Nancy, but now when he held her little left hand she did not withdraw it. They were standing thus, side by side, when Nancy came flying down the stairs.

"Susan!" she called. "Oh, Susan!"

"She is here with me," he said.

Nancy came in breathless. "She came downstairs alone, David! I was helping Ricky. They're in such a hurry they can't get their shoes tied. So she simply came down alone!"

"I know," he said. "She stood there in the doorway. Then she came in. Look—she lets me hold her hand."

"Oh, the darling!" Nancy cried softly, and sat down in a chair opposite the tree. "It's more beautiful than ever, because it's a special Christmas."

At this, Susan withdrew her hand gently and tiptoed to Nancy's side. Then, pointing her forefinger at the tree, she whispered.

"Jolie—pretty?"

"Yes, dear." She lifted the little girl to her lap. "Oh, David, what if they see and *want* her?"

He shook his head, unbelieving, and then they heard the two boys thundering down the stairs to join them.

They all joined hands then and stood around the tree. David led them in singing "Tannenbaum, O Tannenbaum," and he saw Susan softly moving her lips but uttering not a sound. She's doing her best, he thought, her very best to be one of us, bless her.

After that the day burst into its usual happy turmoil, the boys shouting and exulting, asking questions, demanding help.

"Dad, how does this work?"

"Mom, show me how to do this puzzle, please."

And throughout, Susan sat on a small needlepoint stool, her gifts piled about her, opening them gravely one by one, examining each, and putting each in its place in a neat pile on the floor beside her. Ah, but the doll, of course! She had thought it part of the tree, it seemed, for last night they had set it on a branch near the top, securing it with a pink ribbon. Now Nancy cut the ribbon and lifted the doll down, a girl doll, small enough to hold comfortably. She put it in Susan's arms and the child received the gift as a treasure not to be believed.

"C'est pour moi?" she asked under her breath.

"Yes, darling, for you," Nancy said.

Looking at Susan's face, David smiled. "She has what she really wants," he said.

But Susan heard nothing. In the midst of the boys' shouts and laughter, in the midst of the exchange of gifts between the two adults, she sat absorbed, undressing the doll, examining the rubber-skinned body carefully, then dressing it again.

David and Nancy finished opening their gifts and were exchanging a kiss when a man's voice interrupted them.

"A merry Christmas, I'd say—if you can believe what you see!"

They looked up. In the doorway stood Richard and Miranda: snowflakes dotted their shoulders and clung in Miranda's red hair.

"It's snowing again," Miranda said. "We'll have to start home early. But merry Christmas, meanwhile!"

David hurried to greet them and in the hall he helped Miranda with her coat while Richard hung his in the closet. David wanted to be in the room with Nancy when they saw Susan. There might be instant recognition! Nancy was standing in the doorway now. Don't try to hide the child, he thought. It's no use. We must be ready for whatever happens.

"Come into the kitchen," Nancy was saying. "I must put the turkey into the oven. It's a monster—the biggest we've ever had . . . a sort of celebration for our little Susan. It's a special Christmas in this house. I was just saying so. . . ."

She was shepherding Richard and Miranda toward the kitchen, an arm about each, and making talk as she went. "Come on, David, you have to help. I can't lift the bird."

So they were in the kitchen and there was a moment's respite—no, only a delay, and that was no use. Richard and Miranda stood smiling, watching, and Nancy looked away. They were a beautiful pair, she thought, Richard so blond and Miranda a red-haired angel.

They might make good parents for a child! Was David right in not telling them, in not leaving the decision to them? Has any person the right to make a decision for another, even his brother? In her place, were she Miranda, were she Richard, she would say no, let me decide for myself. But she was neither, and Richard was devoted to his career, a dedicated man, a single-minded man, who, if his ambitions were thwarted, would be destroyed. David had pointed that out to her again and again.

"If it were I," David had said, "I'd want to know. But then I'm not a single-minded man. Nor do I want a career in politics. There's nothing I couldn't leave, except my family. I'm a lawyer, yes, but a small-town lawyer. I can do a dozen other things—real estate, for example. Sure, I love my home, and it would hurt me to leave—but then I wouldn't leave. I'd just say to the neighbors, yes, I was a kid in Vietnam once upon a time. Nancy's my wife and she wants the child!"

David had taken Nancy's hand. "But Miranda wouldn't want the child, Nancy—you know that. She'd care about what people said. She and Richard would both be broken up. I know my own brother, as fine a fellow as ever lived, but—well. I know him. He's on his way up, and I can't take the responsibility of blocking that upward way. People are sticky about a man's past, if he's dreaming of a Washington career. I know there's no limit to Richard's dreams, and I know he's the caliber the nation needs."

Nancy had listened to this, had allowed herself to be convinced. Now she was unconvinced again. Oh, let the day take its course! If the child were recognized, then let it be so. If not—oh pray God, it's not!

"Come and see the children," she said brightly when the turkey was in. She led the way bravely, and David stepped ahead to her side.

"Susan is engrossed with her doll," he said. "Don't mind if she makes no response just now. She's a single-minded little soul."

Susan did not look up when the two couples came in. She was undressing her doll again, folding

253

each small garment carefully as she took it off. The boys jumped to their feet.

"Uncle Richard——"

"Aunt Miranda——"

Miranda fended off Ricky, laughing. "Careful, Ricky, I've put on my best dress for you——"

Richard said, "Hi there, Jimmy," and sides ripped the violent embrace.

"Susan," Nancy called. "Come here, dear. This is Aunt Miranda."

Nancy went to the little girl, put the now naked doll into her arms, and led her forward.

"Aunt Miranda," she repeated distinctly. "And Uncle Richard."

Nancy glanced at David as she spoke and caught his solemn gaze. Now was the moment.

"What a pretty child," Miranda said. "How do you do, Susan?" She leaned and touched her lips to Susan's cheek.

Ricky interrupted. "Did you bring us presents, Aunt Miranda?"

"Oh, Ricky," Nancy said. "For shame!"

"For shame," Jimmy echoed. "But you always do, don't you, Uncle Richard?"

"Of course," the uncle said. "Only this time it's a present so big I have to have help. It's for both of you."

"I'll help!" Jimmy shouted.

"Me too," Ricky cried.

"Richard," Miranda said. "You haven't spoken to Susan!"

He had turned to the door but now he looked over his shoulder, the boys clinging to his legs.

"Hi there, Susan," he said. "All right, fellows, come on and help."

He went out to the car, David and the boys following, and Miranda sat down and smoothed her short skirt.

"We spent the night in Boston," she told Nancy. "Richard wanted to push through in one day, but I can't take such a long day, especially with the next day Christmas, which is always a little tiring with children, I find. You really must come to us next year, Nancy. You'd enjoy Washington."

"The children are used to being here at Christmas," Nancy said gently. "But it's sweet of you to think of us. And we'll understand if it becomes too difficult for you to get away."

She was watching Miranda's stone-gray eyes. No, Miranda never glanced at Susan. The little girl had gone back to her chair and was dressing the doll again. Her bright hair fell straightly on each side of her face, hiding it in shadow. But Miranda was looking out of the window. The snow was falling fast.

❖

Miranda stirred in her chair. "We must start back early," she said. "Else we'll never make Boston tonight. We reserved the hotel room."

"Vermont keeps her roads open very well," Nancy said. Strange how quickly she and Miranda fell out of something to talk about! She was glad when the boys came back again, followed by the two men, carrying a huge box.

"Look!" Ricky shouted. "A train!"

"An electric train," Jimmy corrected.

"Wonderful!" Nancy breathed. "It'll take the rest of the day to put it up."

"Where?" David asked, after a quick look at Nancy. Nothing had happened, he realized. So far so good!

"How about the playroom downstairs?" Nancy suggested.

"Oh, no," Ricky protested. "We want it here by the tree."

"Just for today," David said. "We'll move it to-morrow."

"Not too difficult after we have the thing assembled," Richard said.

Richard never looked at Susan, now buttoning the doll's dress. She has nimble fingers, Nancy thought; Susan did everything with a careful perfection. Oh, really, she could not spare this child!

The snow fell softly through the long morning until noon, and then stopped. The sun slanted its way through the clouds and dispelled them. The scent of roasting turkey drifted through the house as the two women set the table with Nancy's best silver and china, and decorated it with sprigs of holly.

"Party favors, as usual, for the children," Nancy said, "but when the crackers pop I hope Susan won't be frightened."

"She hasn't left off playing with that doll all morning," Miranda said. "I wish I'd had time to get the child a present, Nancy, but we didn't get your letter saying she was here until Christmas Eve and you know what it's like to shop then."

"She doesn't miss it," Nancy said.

"A queer-looking little thing, with that Asian face and that light hair."

"We think she's beautiful," Nancy said.

"She doesn't talk much, does she?"

"Of course, she does—perfect French and already beginning in English."

"Was she homesick?"

"No. She was told she was coming home—to us."

"What about her mother?"

"She's dead."

"Are there a lot of these children?"

❖

"Many, we're told."

"So that's what our men are so busy about abroad!"

"Not all of them, I'm sure. . . . Does Richard like his salad with the turkey?"

"He doesn't like salad, period. Remember?"

"Ah, I'd forgotten. . . . Now everything is ready, I think. I love Christmas dinner."

"I'm sorry that you can't have it at night——"

"Oh, midafternoon is the only time if there're children. They get too tired playing all day and then if they have a big dinner. . . ."

Idle talk, she thought, but somehow there was never much else to talk about with Miranda. But perhaps she was to blame, for Miranda had been a writer for a woman's page before she was married, and she, Nancy, had never been anything but David's wife. Did she feel a slight inferiority to this smart woman from Washington? No, she did not!

"Dinner!" she called into the living room. "The turkey can't wait."

They all came out then to the dining room, the boys reluctant to leave their toys.

"We have the track assembled and the engine working," David reported. He lifted Susan into her chair. "And this afternoon we'll get the train moving. You must have spent a pretty penny, Richard."

"It was fun," Richard said briefly.

"A beautiful set," David said.

He glanced at Nancy and shook his head slightly. Nothing, he conveyed to her inquiring eyes—nothing at all. He didn't look at the child.

"Everyone sit down," David said. "And no one may talk while I carve the bird. It takes concentration and skill! And loving care."

"What's loving care, Daddy?" Ricky inquired.

"It means to go slow and take it as it comes," David said. He sharpened the carving knife meticulously and then all eyes were on him as the first slice was carved, brown-skinned on top and white inside.

All eyes, that is, except Miranda's. She was gazing at Susan, who sat at Nancy's side.

"I declare," Miranda said suddenly. "That child looks enough like the boys to be their sister—the same blond hair, the same color eyes!"

Richard looked at Susan. "You're right," he said. He laughed. "And don't look at me, please, Miranda! There were thousands of American boys over there and a lot of them had light hair and eyes."

Miranda laughed. "Thank God for that!"

"Thank God, anyway," David said, gravely. Again his eyes met Nancy's at the end of the table. Steady, he was saying to her, steady now.

"Here's your plate, Miranda," he said. "You're the first to be served."

Miranda took her plate, forgetting the child, and neither she nor Richard saw what Susan did, nor heard what she said. Under Miranda's half-idle stare Susan had put out her hand to Nancy.

"Merci, Mama," she whispered.

"I'm here, Susan," Nancy said. Putting out her own hand she clasped the small searching one. "Mama's here."

The Bells of Christmas Eve

❅

JOE WHEELER

Two women sat at the feet of Christ: Mary and Martha. There is something in most of us that identifies with the beautiful Mary—so effusive, appreciative, responsive, and filled with the joy of life!

But there was the second sister, not nearly so flamboyant, whose love manifested itself not in mere rhetoric but in service. It is the Marthas among us who carry on their shoulders the burdens of the world. It is the Marthas who nurture and sustain the eagles who fly so perilously close to the sun.

But Marthas have their dreams, too.

❊ ❊ ❊

"When will the bells ring?"

"Midnight, Miss Louisa . . . midnight."

"Thank you, Jacques. I'll . . . I'll be waiting. Don't forget the carriage."

"I won't, Miss Louisa."

She turned and walked to the hotel window, leaned against the sill, and waited. Waited, as was her custom, for the dying of the day. She sighed with a faint feeling of loss, for the sudden disappearance of the silver path to the sun that had so recently spanned the deep blue Mediterranean sea and sky.

Losing all track of time, her soul's lens recorded on archival film every detail as the master scene painter of the universe splashed all the colors and hues on His palette across the gilding sky. At the peak of intensity, she felt like a child again, watching that last heart-stopping explosion of fireworks that transforms mundane evening darkness into a twilight of the gods.

Then, as suddenly as it had come, it was over—
and the curtain of night was drawn down to the dark-
ening sea.

It was only then that the icy blade of loneliness
slashed across her heart . . . and time ceased to be.

How much time passed before awareness returned, she
never knew, for the breakers of awareness came in soft
and slow, seemingly in unison with those breaking on
the French Riviera shore outside the window.

Fully awakened at last, she slipped into her heavy
coat, stepped outside, and walked across lawn and sand
to her favorite rocky shelf. After snuggling down into
a natural hollow out of the path of the winter wind, she
spread her coat over her legs and wrapped a small blanket around her shoulders.

The tide was ebbing now, and with its departure
she again realized how terribly lonely were the shores
of her inner world . . . If only *he* were here to hold
her, to commune with her, to fill that void in her life
that only he could fill, achieve that sense of complete-
ness that only he could induce.

Scenes from the past summer flashed on the
screens of her mind: his arrival in a huge carriage at the
Pension Victoria; her almost instant recognition of his

weakened health; his stories detailing his involvement in the ill-fated Polish revolt against Russian tyranny, his capture and incarceration in a damp airless dungeon, and his eventual release.

Fresh from her service as a nurse in Washington during the recent American Civil War, she noted the same battle symptoms that marked tens of thousands of her own countrymen: the tell-tale signs of a weakened constitution, and the lingering evidence of recent illness and almost unendurable stress and pain. Instinctively, she steered the newcomer over to a table near the largest porcelain stove. That simple act of kindness supplied the spark that short-circuited the stuffy formalities of the day: one moment they were complete strangers; a moment later they were friends.

She was a 33-year-old June to his 21-year-old April. But hers was a young-at-heart 33, and his a maturity far beyond his years, forged by the crucible of war and imprisonment. But it was his seared, but cheerful still, spirit that won her heart. In spite of his recent residence in hell, this bruised and tattered lark was a living embodiment of the poetical portrayal of two men looking out through selfsame bars, one seeing walls, the other stars. Ladislas Wisniewiski saw the stars.

Used to the cold formality and austerity of New

England, she was totally unprepared for warmhearted Ladislas, who smashed through conventions and formalities as though they were so much kindling, a Mozart minuet stormed by a Liszt rhapsody.

In truth, Louisa had been the object of many a lovesick swain through the years, but none had been able to break through her self-imposed barriers of reserve and indifference; prior to Ladislas, not one had been able to raise her temperature so much as one degree.

The days and evenings that followed were full of adventures, large and small. He taught her French and she taught him English; he regaled her with the culture, history, and lore of the alpine country of Switzerland and France, and she introduced him to the New World of America; they rowed almost daily on beautiful Lake Geneva, framed by the snowcapped Alps; they explored the grounds of the chateau and area sights of interest such as the nearby Castle of Chillon, which Byron had immortalized; they took frequent tramps along the mountain sides, pausing often to drink in the stunning deep blue sheet of water spread out below them, the verdant hills around them, and the sawtooth mountains above them, cutting notches in the sky.

And woven into the fabric of that never-to-be-forgotten summer of '65 was talk—talk when talk added color, silence when talk was superfluous. Their talk recognized no barriers, no constraints. The subject was life, life with all its complexities, inequities, and unanswered questions. In the evenings, Ladislas would perform in the parlor (he was an accomplished professional musician), and Louisa would join the others and listen. Deep, deep within her, seas long dead would be stirred into tempests by Ladislas's fomenting fingers.

He was good for her—far better than she knew, for Louisa was (and always had been) a caregiver, a Martha, one who sublimated her own dreams and desires so others could fulfill theirs. All her life, others had always come first. She had grown up early, realizing while yet a child that it was her beloved mother who bore the full weight of the family's financial problems, for her father—bless him!—seemingly dwelt in another world. Like Dickens' immortal Micawber, he blithely assumed that something would always "turn up" to enable the family to muddle through. Certainly, God would provide. Somehow, some way, God always did, but in the process her mother, Abba, grew old before her time.

Louisa had early recognized that she, by nature and temperament, was born to be an extension of her mother. She had sometimes resisted and resented this burden, but not for long, for hers was a sunny disposition; duty was not an ugly Puritan word but something you shouldered with a song in your heart.

Rummaging around in her mind, Louisa took off a dusty cobwebby shelf a Christmas reel of her childhood: images of that bitterly cold New England winter flooded the walls of memory. They were down to their last few sticks of wood, and the winter wind howled around the snow-flocked house, icy fingers reaching in through every crack and crevice and chink. Besides the three sisters, a newborn was now at risk when the firewood was gone. "God will provide," was her father's rejoinder to his wife's worried importuning. "God will provide as He always has."

Just then, there was a knock on the door. A neighbor had braved the banshee winds to bring over a load of wood, unable to escape the conviction that the family needed firewood. "Needed firewood?" Abba's face resembled a rainbow on a golden morning.

Later that memorable evening, Father had disappeared for some time. When he returned, stomping his half-frozen feet on the fireside hearth to restore circulation, he jubilantly announced that another neighbor, with a sick baby in a near-freezing house, had asked for help—how providential that the Lord had sent his family wood. Abba's face grew coldly pale: "You . . . you didn't . . . certainly, you *didn't!*" But she knew even before he answered that he had. How *could* he? *They* had a baby too! This was just more than flesh and blood could bear.

But before her pent-up wrath could erupt there was another knock on the door—and another load of wood waited outside. "I told you that we would not suffer," was her father's trusting response. Abba and her girls just looked at each other, absolutely mute.

Louisa stirred, aware of a change in the tide: it was beginning to return. A dream-like full moon had risen, and the breakers were now luminous with a ghostly beauty. The wind had died down at last.

Truant-like, before she knew they had slipped away, her thoughts returned to that golden summer in Vevey. How lonely she had been. At first, the mere idea of seeing Europe had entranced her; all she had to do was care for a family friend's invalid daughter: be a

❦

companion. But the girl was so insensitive to the beauty and history Louisa revelled in that her *joie de vivre* had begun to fade.

And then came Ladislas.

He filled a long-aching void in her life, for, growing up, she had been so tall, coltish, and tomboyish that romance could be found only in storybooks and in dreams. Her sisters were the soft, the feminine, the lovely ones.

Then, when she had grown up, this ugly-duckling self-image refused to go away, in spite of the refutation in her mirror and in the eyes of men. As a result, she remained shy and unsure of herself—and certainly, so far, success in her chosen career was mighty slow in coming.

Ladislas had unlocked an inner Louisa that even she had never seen before. Free for the first time in her life to be young without heavy responsibilities and worries, her day-by-day interactions with Ladislas brought new gentleness and vivacity to her face, and his open adoration, stars to her eyes. The older travelers staying at the pension watched the couple, subconsciously envying their youth and happiness. In the evening, in the flickering candlelight, Louisa's face was graced by that inner radiance that comes but once in a woman's life: from the full knowledge that she is loved and adored by the man she perceives to be her world.

She borrowed not from the future but accepted each day, each hour, each minute, as a gift from God. The realities of life were swept aside to dissipate in the mists of the mountains as they lived each moment with the intensity of those who live on the slopes of a volcano or on an earthquake fault. Time enough for harsh realities later, when the cherubims of circumstance barred them from Eden with their flaming swords.

But like all Shan-gri-las, this one too had to end. As the cool autumn winds swept down from Mont Blanc, Louisa's invalid charge decided it was time to move to a warmer climate—southern France would be ideal.

Louisa tearfully packed her trunks. It was no longer possible to pretend that this idyllic island in time would be their home. The age differential, Ladislas's lack of livelihood prospects and his weakened health, their cultural differences, Louisa's commitments to her family as well as her own career uncertainties—and, of course, the slight tincture of the maternal in her love for him—all added up to a gradually growing conviction that it would never be. Even as they rowed together, it was her sister, May, whom she

272

envisioned opposite Ladislas down through the years; her age equating with his, her love of music and art responding to his, her infectious love of life feeding upon his boyish blandishments, impulsiveness, and warm and tender heart.

But none of this took away from the bittersweet parting. Masking his intense feeling, he kissed her hand in the European manner. As she watched his waving scarf recede into a blur down the train tracks, her eyes filled with tears.

For what right had she to dream of marriage? She who had vowed to shore up her mother's failing strength, assisting her in every way possible; and then, when that beloved caregiver could no longer function very well, quietly and cheerfully taking her place.

Then, too, Louisa vaguely realized that she was out of step with most of the women of her age, in that marriage, children, and domesticity was really not her, all in all. For she had career dreams of her own, and had little inclination to turn over her life to a man, becoming old before her time by repeated pregnancies and brutally heavy housework.

But even that could not check the tears running down her cheeks . . . for love is not governed by the mind.

She pulled out her watch and, by the light of the climbing moon, discovered it was almost 11. Just before midnight, she planned to take a carriage to the ancient cathedral and see the nativity scene everyone had been talking about. She hungered to hear the choir and pipe organ celebrate the birth of Jesus 18 and a half centuries ago.

In her pocket was a letter from home (worn and tattered from many readings) that her fingers touched in the darkness. She had no need to reread it for she knew it by heart: Father's lecture tours were not doing very well; Anna had just given birth to her second son (how good John was to her!); Mother continued to weaken, her gradual buckling to the resistless juggernaut of the years becoming ever more apparent to the writer of the letter, May; and as for May—how much she needed a chance to flower, to become a real artist: she must be given the opportunity to experience Europe, too.

And never far from mind was Beth—little Beth with her endearing ways, whose untimely death seven years before had left an aching void that time would never fill or completely heal. What a *dear* family she had! And how they loved each other! Wouldn't it be wonderful if she could use her writing talents to somehow recapture those magical childhood years, so permeated with sunlight and shadows, laughter and tears.

But every story, especially a story of four girls, has to have a hero, too. Perhaps——the image of a dark-haired Polish musician, forever teasing, laughing, and cajoling . . . She could no more resist him than she could the incoming tide now lapping at her feet. Brother, sweetheart, and friend. But "Ladislas" would never do. Um-m . . . how about "Lawrence" . . . but she'd call him "Laurie."

She sank into a reverie outside the stream of time. She had no way of foreseeing the future: of knowing that four months later, "Laurie" would be waiting for her at the train station, and that for two wonderful weeks he, she, and Paris in the spring would coalesce in memories that would never die. Nor could she know that three years later, her book, the first half of the story, would be published, and a year after that, the second-half sequel would be snapped up by a constantly growing audience. The book would become the most beloved story ever written about an American girl. For, in spite of all her efforts to show off her sisters, offsetting their portraits with unvarnished depictions of her own frailties, mistakes, and weaknesses, she would fail in her purpose——for it would be Jo with whom generations of readers would fall in love.

❖

And who among us could ever read that unforgettable passage, set in the eternally flowering gardens of Vevey, wherein Amy, still mourning the recent death of her sister Beth, looks up . . . and sees him standing there:

> Dropping everything, she ran to him, exclaiming, in a tone of unmistakable love and longing, 'Oh, Laurie, Laurie, I knew you'd come to me!'

Yes, who among us could ever read that without sensing that the words were really Jo's, that the broken heart was really Jo's, and that the longing for a love that would forever remain imprisoned in the bud of might-have-been, never blossoming into the rose of marriage, was Jo's. Who among us can read that heartbroken call without tears?

"Miss Louisa? . . . uh, Miss Alcott?"

"Uh . . . I'm sorry, Jacques, I guess I . . . I must have dozed off. What is it?"

"You asked me to have the carriage ready at 15 minutes before midnight."

"Oh, yes! Thank you—just give me a minute."

Soon Louisa was settled within the carriage. The horses snorted in the cold night air, and the wheels complained as they chattered and clattered over cobblestone streets. She looked out her window and took in the festive crowd and air of expectancy that hovered over the city. She realized that she regretted nothing—even if she had the opportunity to live her life over again she would change not one line. Joy and pain, hand-in-hand—without both she would have but a one-dimensional ditty or dirge; with both, a multifaceted symphony of life.

She could ask for no more.

Then she heard them, faint at first, soon gathering power as they were joined by other bells across the city. The crescendo continued until the ringing and the clanging swallowed up every other sound on earth.

It was Christmas . . . Christ was born in a manger.

Written December 1990. I am deeply indebted to Cornelia Meigs, for without her moving Invincible Louisa, *with its invaluable biographical material and discussion of the evolution of* Little Women, *this story would never have been. And I must not forget my American literature class at Columbia Union College—it was the lecture I wrote for them that inspired this story.*

A NOTE FROM THE EDITORS

This book was selected by the Book and Inspirational Media Division of the company that publishes *Guideposts*, a monthly magazine filled with true stories of hope and inspiration.

Guideposts is available by subscription. All you have to do is write to Guideposts, 39 Seminary Hill Road, Carmel, New York 10512. When you subscribe, each month you can count on receiving exciting new evidence of God's presence, His guidance and His limitless love for all of us.

Guideposts Books are available on the World Wide Web at www.guidepostsbooks.com. Follow our popular book of devotionals, *Daily Guideposts*, and read excerpts from some of our best-selling books. You can also send prayer requests to our Monday morning Prayer Fellowship and read stories from recent issues of our magazines, *Guideposts, Angels on Earth*, and *Guideposts for Teens*.